A CHALLENGE FOR ACADEMIC LIBRARIES

LIBRARY ORIENTATION SERIES
Sul H. Lee, Editor

82676

Number one: Library Orientation; Papers Presented at
the First Annual Conference on Library Orientation
held at Eastern Michigan University, May 7, 1971.

Number two: A Challenge for Academic Libraries:
How to Motivate Students to Use the Library.

Library Orientation Series — No. 2

A CHALLENGE FOR ACADEMIC LIBRARIES

How to Motivate Students to Use the Library

Edited
and with an Introduction by
SUL H. LEE
Acting Director of the Library
and
Associate Professor
Eastern Michigan University

Published for the
EASTERN MICHIGAN UNIVERSITY LIBRARY
Ypsilanti, Michigan
by
THE PIERIAN PRESS
Ann Arbor, Michigan
1973

Library of Congress Catalog Card No. 73-78295
ISBN 0-87650-039-4

THE PIERIAN PRESS
P.O. Box 1808
Ann Arbor, MI. 48106

TABLE OF CONTENTS

INTRODUCTION

It is apparent that there are more questions which seek answers than practical solutions suggested for the many and varied problems in implementing library orientation programs. The topics frequently discussed during the Second Annual Conference on Library Orientation for Academic Libraries ranged from a simple question of how to start the program to the rather complex question of how worthwhile it all is.

Despite persistent problems, including tenacious confusion in the concept itself, library orientation is still a continuing center of concern because there is no doubt in the minds of many academic librarians that this is clearly an avenue which will lead to meeting the ultimate objective of academic libraries—to bring the user and the information closer together. Better library orientation is fundamental if the user is to have a better map for finding resource materials he needs in the library. As a result, more resources will be available to the user.

With this ambitious mission, librarians look upon the program of library orientation as a great challenge. It is a challenge, not simply because its implementation is a very difficult task, but because it is a tremendously complex process which requires commitment both from librarians themselves and the teaching faculty.

The search for some suggestions in the light of this challenge was one of the obvious themes for the Second Annual Conference. Each of the four papers presented at the Conference makes interesting points and suggests possible solutions for similar environments. This volume is a compilation of these papers. It makes no effort to be a sequel to the proceedings of the First Annual Conference. Instead, it tries to supplement what was already said in that volume.

It is the editor's cherished hope that we will find several keys to successful implementation of library orientation programs through conferences such as this one in which the melting pot of many ideas combines varied experiences of those participants in the Conference. We are already planning the Third Annual Conference which will be held May 3 and 4, 1973.

For the editorial assistance they have rendered, the editor is grateful to Ann Andrew and Robin Branstator of the Eastern Michigan University Library.

Sul. H. Lee

Ann Arbor
February 10, 1973

viii

TRIALS, TACTICS, AND TIMING:
SOME THOUGHTS ON LIBRARY INSTRUCTION PROGRAMS

Mary Jo Lynch
The University of Michigan

Many months ago, when Sul Lee asked me to speak at this conference, I wanted to decline because two questions bothered me. First of all, I wondered about the title of the program, the Second Annual Conference on Library Orientation for Academic Libraries. Most of the academic librarians I know are not worried about library orientation. (I know few junior college librarians, so anything I say here has that limitation.) Academic librarians are well aware that they should plan something to introduce freshmen and other new students to the campus library because these students need an orientation which *Webster's Third New International Dictionary* defines as "an introduction to an unfamiliar situation." Sometimes the vehicle of this orientation is simply a handbook; often this print media is supplemented by a film, video tape, slide/tape presentation, lecture or conducted tour which usually lasts about an hour and shows students where things are in the library building. Of course someone needs to use imagination and intelligence in planning an effective orientation program, but the content of the presentation is fairly obvious and everyone -- faculty, students,

1

administration -- expects the library staff to plan something to show the newcomers where things are.

Some librarians try to do more than this in an orientation program -- to show students how to use the card catalog, for example, or to demonstrate the use of the various periodical indexes. Most who have tried this, however, would probably agree with the conclusion Verna Melum reached after five years as Library Orientation and Instruction Librarian at Northern Illinois University. Melum said: "We have learned that it is futile to present anything beyond the most general information at an introductory lecture to students."[1]

In her 1971 survey of library orientation and instruction programs in libraries across the country which was published in the July & October 1971 issue of the *Drexel Library Quarterly*, Melum reported that others have come to the same conclusion. She found that "much less is being done for freshmen during Orientation Week or in early fall than formerly. *Orientation* is now mainly a welcome. *Instruction* comes later and is continuous."[2]

Evidently many librarians have come to understand the difference between orientation and instruction, but we are still living with the idea that all freshmen can be given an "orientation" to the library which will cover everything they need to know about using libraries during their academic careers. In her article in the July & October 1971 *Drexel Library Quarterly*, Millicent Palmer calls this "The Ghost of Library Instruction Past." She reports that such a ghost was the greatest single problem she encountered in trying to develop an instruction program which would provide bibliographic knowledge to upperclassmen at Southern Illinois University:

The image of library instruction as a single massive inoculation of freshmen

2

against all further needs for information-search knowledge, appears to consciously or subconsciously condition the thinking of most faculty and students.[3]

Today, many academic librarians are convinced that they must banish that ghost because they believe that they have a responsibility to help college students acquire the skills involved in using the many resources of the academic library. This can be done on an individual basis, of course, as reference librarians work with students, but too few students know enough about library resources to realize that a reference librarian would be able to help them with anything more than a factual question or a problem with the card catalog, and reference departments in most academic libraries would be hard pressed to supply more sophisticated assistance if a large number of students asked for it. To overcome both of these difficulties, a few academic librarians have tried to offer instruction to groups of students, not just occasionally, but on an organized basis. They have tried to develop programs which take orientation for granted and go on from there to help students learn how to use the many means which libraries provide to enable users to gain access to recorded knowledge.

Ideally, or so it seems to me, the library staff, working with the faculty, would set up a program which would gradually introduce students to the way information is organized in the various disciplines and in libraries. Patricia Knapp planned an impressive program for Monteith College though it was never completely implemented. Earlham College has been able to work out a program which they describe as "course-related, demonstrated and gradated."[4] But, at this moment, I am not aware of other institutions where a similar program has been

3

worked out. I would guess that it could only be done in a small college.

Some large institutions and some small ones too have developed credit or non-credit courses on the use of library resources. I have heard that the course at Berkeley, for example, is very successful. But it is my impression that, generally, such a course has a very limited appeal, especially if it is non-credit. If the course is to be offered for credit, the library staff has to persuade some faculty committee that the course is legitimate -- an investment of time and energy that few library staffs can afford since the gains (number of students contacted) are usually so small. The practical value of a course on the use of the library is certainly challenged by Verna Melum's statement of "the two major conclusions which run through both of the surveys" of library orientation and instruction which she has made in the last four years (1969 and 1971). Librarians across the country told her: "(1) library instruction is effective only at the time of need and (2) learning to use a library is a continuing process."[5]

To provide this kind of instruction, some institutions, notably Northern Illinois University and Southern Illinois University, have one staff member who spends a major part of her time offering instruction in the use of library resources to classes and letting faculty know that this instruction is available. It seems to me that this is the best that can be hoped for, especially in large institutions. But the idea is not yet widely accepted. Millicent Palmer, who holds the title of Library Instruction Librarian at Southern Illinois, believes that, at present, such persons are "functioning as professional mavericks or orphans, or both" and warns that "persons who dare assume the title, 'Library Instruction Librarian,' do so at their own risk. The only

4

supportive influence is the fact that their administrators are aware of need and have faith in the possibility of solving old problems in new ways."[6]

The new ways are not really revolutionary; what they do is to formalize and extend a practice which has been common in most academic libraries for years, *i.e.* a librarian, usually a reference librarian, talks to a class about the reference tools useful in the study of a particular subject at the request of a faculty member. Why not just continue to let this happen as it has in the past -- occasionally, accidentally, if someone on the library staff has the time and the interest? Some librarians say, by their silence, that we can; others insist that showing students how to use a library is every bit as important as collecting materials, organizing them for use, and answering reference questions for the faculty. It is so important to the educational program of the institution that we cannot just let it happen. We need to have librarians on the staff who work at it exclusively, who are pleasantly aggressive about telling faculty and students what librarians can do, who are creative about planning instructional sessions that are relevant to what a particular group of students is studying, and who do, indeed, help them learn how to make effective use of the resources of the library.

In case you have not heard, that Committee was established and was asked:

...to consider the possibility of establishing a clearinghouse for information on instructional programs currently in operation; to explore methods of evaluating existing programs and materials; and to investigate the need for research into problems connected with instruction programs.[7]

I tried to convince Sul that this conference should be named after that committee because I believe that bibliographic instruction, not orientation, is the problem area in academic libraries. Sul insisted that his idea of orientation could include my idea of instruction and told me I was welcome to concentrate on the latter if I wished.

So I stopped arguing for the moment, but, in the back of my head, something continues to tell me that academic librarians must recognize the difference between orientation to the library and instruction in the use of library resources. If we do not see the difference clearly and say so by what we do and what we do not do, students and faculty will never get the message and students will continue to insist, when we come to a classroom to tell a group about the library resources which will help them solve a particular research problem, "But I've heard the library lecture." The "Ghost of Library Instruction Past" will continue to haunt us.

The second question I presented to Sul was that I did not think I ought to speak since I could not describe a successful, ongoing program as the other speakers would be doing. Last August I retired for a while from the arena of orientation and instruction after spending two frustrating years at the University of Massachusetts trying to establish an instructional program similar to the ones at Northern Illinois and Southern Illinois. I did learn a lot about teaching students how to use libraries, but the visible results were less than spectacular. Sul said that did not matter, that I should just talk about what we tried and what we learned. The people who came to the conference last year told him that what they most appreciated was the opportunity to hear people describe their own experiences, both successes and failures. One can learn

6

from both, of course, and too often, in the literature and at conferences, we hear only about past successes or about exciting plans for the future.

I have no such plans to report to you this morning, but I will try to tell you what I learned while trying to develop a bibliographical instruction program at the University of Massachusetts. Orientation was my responsibility too and I'm afraid I wasted a lot of time and energy on it before I realized, as Verna Melum did, that anything more than a welcome was futile.

I have entitled this speech "Trials, Tactics and Timing," because as I thought about bibliographic instruction I kept thinking about my favorite of Piet Hein's delightful *Grooks*, the one entitled *T. T. T.*:

> Put up in a place
> where it's easy to see
> the cryptic admonishment
>   T. T. T.
>
> When you feel how depressingly
> slowly you climb,
> it's well to remember that
>   Things Take Time.[8]

Trials

Time is, perhaps, the most difficult trial library instruction librarians face. We know we have something to offer, something students need, but it takes time to convince faculty and students and, often, other librarians that this is so. And once we are invited into the classroom, it takes time to prepare an effective presentation -- time supervisors are not always willing to give us because the other business of the library must be taken care of. So T. T. T. ought to be

Put up in a place
where it's easy to see
in the office of every library instruction
librarian.

In some cases, the time problem may be that
the library administration expects you to develop a full blown and successful instructional
program within a few months or a year. Such
unrealistic expectations can be a real burden
since, as any librarian who has worked with
instructional programs knows, such a miracle
is just not possible.

Before the program can begin, faculty must
be convinced that bibliographic instruction
is something they want to incorporate into
their courses. We should have no illusions
about reaching the entire faculty, for as
Patricia Knapp has reminded us "The potential
for active collaboration between the library
and the faculty varies from discipline to discipline as well as from individual to individual."[9] But we do need to find out which
departments and instructors would be most open
to the suggestion that a librarian might help
their students learn how to use library resources. And that takes time and tact and an
understanding of the intellectual climate of
a particular campus.

I have heard academic librarians talk about
reaching students without faculty cooperation,
but I seriously doubt that this approach can
work, except in connection with those very few
students who have time to spare and are curious about how information is organized in libraries. Most students have very little time
left after meeting the demands of class work
and prefer to spend it somewhere else besides
in a library. These students might really
welcome bibliographic instruction if it is
effectively presented and related to the requirements of a particular course, but the

8

course integration is critical. To arrange
that, a librarian needs to work very closely
with faculty and this cannot be done until the
librarian is very familiar with the institution
and has made some personal contacts with members of the teaching staff.

Librarians who have never tried to convince
faculty that students need bibliographic instruction might wonder how we can suggest that
working with faculty is one of our trials.
Surely instructors believe that students should
learn how to investigate a subject independently and surely that means learning to use
library resources, at least in most subjects.
What we are doing is offering to help faculty
educate students; the faculty ought to welcome
us into the classroom. But they do not.

Patricia Knapp's ground-breaking report on
the *Monteith College Library Experiment* explains
why:

> Most college faculty members see library
> instruction as dealing with bits of in-
> formation, undeniably useful, but frag-
> mented, not related to any single,
> coherent framework, not calling for
> problem-solving behavior, for critical
> thinking, for imagination. Most college
> students see it as sheer high school
> busy-work.[10]

John Williamson describes another aspect of
the same problem in his recent article on
"Swarthmore College's 'Teaching Library' Proposals." He tells us:

> Faculty members do not really grasp the
> difference between expert knowledge and
> bibliographic control. They know the
> books of their specialties through long
> years of study. This accretion of
> knowledge is for the most part bound up
> with their interest in a particular
> discipline and from a bibliographic point

9

of view is rather haphazard. Usually faculty members are but dimly aware that the bibliographic aids they commonly use represent merely a small part of a large network of bibliographic controls. The idea is foreign to them that knowledge of books in general rather than knowledge of books in a particular field is not only something that can be acquired but is a worthy discipline in itself. Many have little idea of the range of guides and finding aids that a librarian takes for granted, including such basics as Winchell.[11]

These attitudes on the part of most faculty will not just disappear if we ignore them. It hurts our professional pride to admit that they exist, but unless we do so, we will never be able to communicate intelligently with the faculty. Recognizing them may also stimulate us to respond to the challenge Patricia Knapp posed in her "Guidelines for Bucking the System." She notes that "the faculty has limited understanding of the intellectual processes involved in sophisticated library competence" and adds that librarians also have a long way to go: "Since we are far from secure in our own understanding of the intellectual processes in library use, we must also strive to overcome this weakness by attempting constantly to identify and make explicit these processes in our work."[12]

Another trial which must be faced by an academic librarian interested in providing bibliographic instruction to students is that other librarians on the staff, sometimes major administrators, do not believe that bibliographical instruction is important. Librarians who do not work actively with students assume that students learn how to use library resources in a particular field as part of the study of that field. Most reference librarians know that this rarely happens at the undergrad- level and often does not happen at the master's degree level either.

An administrator who does not realize this, however, is not easily convinced that a bibli- graphical instruction program should be in- augurated. But unless top administration supports the program fully by freeing the li- brary instruction librarian from other duties and making it possible for that librarian to have the space and secretarial help and coop- eration from other librarians which are neces- sary for a successful bibliographic instruction program, the program will be very difficult to establish and to develop. If the position is not full time, the library instruction librar- ian may discover that his or her supervisor and colleagues in the department think that the other duties are much more important and view time spent on instruction as time wasted on non-essentials.

The most severe trial a library instruction librarian faces, however, is one we do not like to admit. The fact is, we do not really know what students need to know about libraries and how we can best help them to learn these things. We know what librarians know about libraries, and we sometimes try to teach students that. But undergraduates do not need to learn it, and very little research has been done on just what they do need to learn and how to teach it. Patricia Knapp made a major contribution to our knowledge in this area, but she would be the first to admit that the Monteith pro- ject was just a beginning. Mary Stillman, who wrote "A Program for Action" to conclude *Drexel Library Quarterly's* issue on "Integrating the Library Instruction in the College Curriculum" insists that research must be part of this program. She says:

11

There is now sufficient observation to
formulate hypotheses which can be tested,
and assumptions can be replaced with
knowledge. Research should concern itself with basic, not secondary factors.
For example, why concern ourselves with
whether freshman orientation can be taught
better by computer assisted instruction,
if we have not proven the necessity or
advisability of freshman orientation.
We should not allow our interest in educational technology to divert our attention from educational psychology and the
basic learning process.[13]
The ACRL Ad Hoc Committee on Bibliographic
Instruction plans to study what research is
needed and how it could be done in the near
future.   Undoubtedly they would welcome suggestions from anyone who has ideas about what
should be studied or suggestions as to who
should be asked to do the research and how it
might be funded.

Tactics

So these are the trials one faces when one
becomes involved with bibliographical instruction.   What tactics can a library instruction
librarian use to overcome the obstacles in the
path of a successful bibliographic instruction
program?   This morning I would like to suggest
to you some tactics that I know will work because I have tried them and others that I believe would work even though I have not yet
used them myself.
First of all, learn all you can about what
has happened and is happening in other academic
libraries.   Usually a program must be tailor-
made for your own campus, but much can be
learned from the trials and errors of others.
Librarians who have already done what you want

to do can be quoted as experts when you are trying to convince other librarians that bibliographical instruction is something your library can and should offer. Unfortunately, this has been much easier said than done, but things are looking up. These conferences at EMU and similar conferences in other parts of the country during the last few years are steps in the right direction. So is the July and October 1971 issue of the *Drexel Library Quarterly*. So are the clearinghouses to be established by the New York Library Association at Jefferson Community College,[14] by EMU and by the ACRL Ad Hoc Committee on Bibliographic Instruction.

Just as important as learning about bibliographical instruction programs on other campuses is learning whatever you can about the students and faculty on your own campus. The library instruction librarian needs to get to know the institution thoroughly: study the catalog, the official publications, the student publications; attend meetings of the faculty senate, the student body, faculty and/or student groups concerned with campus issues; work on university committees; have lunch, coffee, cocktails, not always with your colleagues from the library, but often with faculty and students. Be as much a part of the university community as possible. In time you will know which departments and instructors might be interested in discussing bibliographical instruction with you. Offering bibliographical services to campus offices and groups is another way to demonstrate that the academic library is an active service institution, not just a passive warehouse. Funny how people still need to be convinced that there have been some changes made.

It is possible, of course, to advertise the availability of bibliographic instruction in

13

such things as library handbooks and newsletters, but most faculty do not respond to this approach. They need to be contacted directly; but how does one decide which of several hundred faculty one should contact? Personal contacts are some help as are course descriptions. Reference librarians can also be a very valuable source of leads, since the nature and number of questions asked at the reference desk often indicate that a particular class needs bibliographic instruction. At the University of Massachusetts a memo was sent to all reference librarians asking them to be alert to questions which indicated that a whole class needed instruction in the use of library resources. When they were asked such questions, reference librarians were requested to find out as much as possible about the assignment--the exact statement of the problem, the instructor who assigned it, the course, the department. If the student had a copy of a teacher's instructions, the reference librarian would make a copy of it. This information was to be given to the librarian in charge of instructional services who would then contact the faculty member involved about bibliographical instruction, if not for the current class then to future groups who might be assigned similar problems. This approach was only mildly successful when I was at the University of Massachusetts, but I believe it could be a very useful part of a bibliographical instruction program.

Make it clear to all concerned that bibliographical instruction is not orientation. You may be the librarian who is also in charge of whatever program is devised to help newcomers become familiar with the library, but do whatever you can to convince students and faculty and other librarians that orientation is just a welcome and that it is bibliographical instruction which teaches students how to use the library.

When you do contact faculty members, try to be very sympathetic to the problems teachers face in facilitating learning. Organizing the sequence of topics to be discussed in the class meetings of a term, planning meaningful assignments, choosing a text which is worth the money it costs or developing a reading list of materials the student can find easily in the library -- all are things a teacher must give careful thought to, especially now when students are so critical of teachers and the public is asking questions about what is happening in higher education. A librarian who does not understand the teacher's difficulties or is inflexible about when he or she can meet a class, is just another burden to a busy instructor. I highly recommend teaching a course, especially in one's own institution, to any librarian who wants to offer bibliographical instruction to other teachers.

Once this offer has been accepted, the library instruction librarian has the chance to use the most important tactic of all: be so good at bibliographical instruction that you present material which really helps students achieve the objectives of the course. Always remember that it is those objectives, not some abstract ability to use the library, which are important to students and faculty. Ask the instructor for the name of the text and for copies of the course syllabus, the reserve list, the list of topics students will be investigating in the library. Study all of these and plan to demonstrate the use of particular reference tools by explaining a sample entry related to a topic covered by the course or proposed as a term paper topic. It is helpful to come to class with slides or transparencies or Xerox copies of the pages you will be discussing so that students will be able to see what you are talking about when you tell them that a particular reference tool contains a specific kind of information. Advertising brochures from publishers can sometimes be very useful visual aids too. What is important is that students do better work as a result of the librarian's bibliographical instruction. Maybe they will even write their own term papers instead of buying them from Creative Communications, Inc.!

You may need to devote some of your free time to preparing for instructional sessions, especially when the program is just beginning and others in the library are not convinced that it should begin at all. But the careful planning is important enough to the ultimate success of the program that it is well worth this extra effort. If students think your instruction was "relevant," faculty will very likely ask you back. And word may spread to other members of the faculty that there are people in the library who know something about scholarship and are willing to help students. Let's face it: this is often a surprise to teachers.

Once the classroom instruction is finished, the library instruction librarian should be available to students when they come to the library to work on a project. Listening to a talk about reference tools, even a very good talk, is not the same as working with these tools, and some students will need more help. The librarian who gave the bibliographical instruction to the class is probably the best one to provide such assistance.

Find out the subject specialties of other librarians on the staff. You may need to ask them for help if and when you get a request from a teacher in a subject about which you know nothing. A librarian who knows the field well can help you prepare for the instruction or, perhaps, visit the class for you.

Timing

Timing is really one of the tactics I want to suggest to you, but I chose to deal with it separately so that this talk could be built around three "t"'s and so that I could focus on some matters which are often neglected in talk about instructional programs. Timing is important, first of all, in relation to approaching the library administration with plans for a bibliographical instruction program. A new program and one which requires much staff time will not be welcomed when the library is in the middle of reorganization or is implementing other new programs or is moving into new quarters. You will have better luck if you wait until other problems have been solved before you approach library administrators with plans for a bibliographical instruction program.

Meanwhile, of course, lay a solid groundwork for the program by getting to know faculty and students and curriculum and by offering bibliographical instruction on occasion. But any attempt to establish an extensive program should wait until the library can afford to give you the support you will need--your time, the time of other librarians, secretarial help, audio/visual equipment. If the library administration should approach you with the suggestion that you start an extensive program at a time when they cannot give you such support, you had best make it clear to them that very little can be accomplished.

Timing is very important, also, in approaching the faculty. If the relationship between the faculty and the library is not good, you are better off to wait until it improves (and,

of course, work at improving it) before you
try to sell the library as anything more than
a warehouse. When approaching individual
faculty, it is important to be aware of the
way a course is planned and conducted. Often
a professor cannot rearrange his plans for a
particular term, though he may be happy to
agree to work with you the next time the course
is offered. Once you have discovered an instructor who does want you to provide bibliographical instruction for a class, you need
to be flexible about when you can meet the
class and willing to come at a time when you
would not ordinarily be working.

One thing you should *not* be flexible about,
however, is coming to a class only when the
students need bibliographical instruction because they have just been given an assignment
which will require them to use library resources. Occasionally a teacher may think that a
talk about the library would be "good" for
students even though he does not intend to
give them an assignment which will send them
to use the library. Visiting a class under
these circumstances is actually counterproduc-
tive because you will bore most of the students
and thus create a negative image of the library -- an image you or some other librarian
will have to overcome if you should meet those
same students at a later date. So go only to
students who will need to use the library in
the very near future, and schedule the bibliographic instruction at a time when they know
what the assignment will be but before they
have been frustrated by the library. Once
that happens you have real problems convincing
them that libraries are logical, likable
places.

J.-J. Servan-Schreiber, whose 1967 best
seller *The American Challenge* contended that
the major reason American industry expanded

so rapidly since 1930 is that Americans devote so much time and money to education, chose as the epigraph for his book a Chinese saying:
If you give a man fish,
he will have a single meal.
If you teach him how to fish,
he will eat all his life.[15]
That could be another motto to be framed and hung in the office of every library instruction librarian. The skeptic will say that the waters are too polluted and the lines are too tangled, but you have come here today because you believe that academic librarians can and should help students learn how to exploit the resources of your libraries. Let us continue to believe that, and to work hard, remembering that in bibliographical instruction as in fishing, Things Take Time.

Notes

1. Verna Melum, "Library Instruction in a University," *Illinois Libraries*, LI (June, 1969), 520.
2. Verna Melum, "1971 Survey of Library Orientation and Instruction Programs," *Drexel Library Quarterly*, VII (July & October, 1971), 227-228.
3. Millicent Palmer, "Library Instruction at Southern Illinois University, Edwardsville," *Drexel Library Quarterly*, VII (July & October, 1971), 257.
4. James R. Kennedy, Jr., Thomas G. Kirk, and Gwendolyn A. Weaver, "Course-Related Library Instruction; A Case Study of the English and Biology Departments at Earlham College," *Drexel Library Quarterly*, VII (July & October, 1971), 279.
5. Melum, "1971 Survey," p. 227.
6. Palmer, "Library Instruction," p. 255.

19

7. *ALA Handbook of Organization* (Chicago: ALA, 1972), p. 36.
8. Piet Hein, *Grooks* (London: Hodder Paperbacks, 1966), p. 5.
9. Patricia B. Knapp, "Guidelines for Bucking the System: A Strategy for Moving Toward the Ideal of the Undergraduate Library As a Teaching Instrument," *Drexel Library Quarterly*, VII (July & October, 1971), 218.
10. Patricia B. Knapp, *The Monteith College Library Experiment* (New York: Scarecrow Press, 1966), p. 89.
11. John G. Williamson, "Swarthmore College's 'Teaching Library' Proposals," *Drexel Library Quarterly*, VII (July & October, 1971), 210-211.
12. Knapp, "Guidelines," p. 218.
13. Mary E. Stillman, "A Program for Action," *Drexel Library Quarterly*, VII (July & October, 1971), 377.
14. Letter from Arthur P. Young, Vice President, College and University Libraries Section, NYLA to Jean Coleman, Chairman, ALA Committee on Instruction in the Use of Libraries.
15. J.-J. Servan-Schreiber, *The American Challenge* (New York: Atheneum, 1968).

A SCIENTIFIC MODEL FOR THE DEVELOPMENT OF LIBRARY USE INSTRUCTIONAL PROGRAMS

Marvin E. Wiggins
Brigham Young University

Once upon a time a Sea Horse gathered up his seven pieces of eight and cantered out to find his fortune. Before he had traveled very far he met an Eel, who said,

"Psst. Hey, bud. Where 'ya goin'?"

"I'm going out to find my fortune," replied the Sea Horse, proudly.

"You're in luck," said the Eel. "For four pieces of eight you can have this speedy flipper, and then you'll be able to get there a lot faster."

"Gee, that's swell," said the Sea Horse, and paid the money and put on the flipper and slithered off at twice the speed. Soon he came upon a Sponge, who said,

"Psst. Hey, bud. Where 'ya goin'?"

"I'm going out to find my fortune," replied the Sea Horse.

"You're in luck," said the Sponge. "For a small fee I will let you have this jet-propelled scooter so that you will be able to travel a lot faster."

So the Sea Horse bought the scooter

with his remaining money and went zooming
thru the sea five times as fast.   Soon
he came upon a Shark, who said,
     "Psst. Hey, bud. Where 'ya goin'?"
     "I'm going out to find my fortune,"
replied the Sea Horse.
     "You're in luck. If you'll take this
short cut," said the Shark, pointing to
his open mouth,   you'll save yourself a
lot of time."
     "Gee, thanks," said the Sea Horse,
and zoomed off into the interior of the
Shark, there to be devoured.
     The moral of this fable is that if
you're not sure where you're going, you're
liable to end up someplace else.[1]

The major difficulty in designing library
use instructional programs is that one is not
sure where he is going and exactly what end
result he hopes to attain. A need for instruction in the use of libraries has been so apparent that thousands of projects have been at-
tempted.   However, the percentage and degree
of effectiveness have frequently been low.
The purpose of this paper is to present a
carefully defined procedure calling for definition of objectives and containing built - in
guarantees for reaching those objectives.
     For purposes of illustration, reference
will be made to the experience of the Clark
Library of Brigham Young University where such
an instrumental development model has been
employed. A summary of the phases of development of this model is shown in Table I.[2]
     During the summer of 1970, the Clark Library
reference personnel desired to improve its
program for instruction in the use of the library.   Because of dissatisfaction with most
programs in existence at that time, it was
decided to turn to the expertise among the

INSTRUCTIONAL DEVELOPMENT MODEL

Instructional Development Program
Division of Instructional Services - Brigham Young University

TABLE I

University faculty and staff in formulating a series of instructional programs that would indeed work.

A group of consultants including librarians, English instructors, instructional psychologists, and nonprint media experts were called together to examine the educational needs and requirements for providing library use instruction and to make recommendations for the type of programs that would fill that need. It was decided that a centralized program should be established where all lower-division students would receive a series of basic instructional packages that would meet their needs at their level of study.

Inasmuch as English classes were already teaching basic library techniques and were reaching nearly all students of the University, the English composition department was involved as a key source in determining the content of basic library instruction.

Letters of support were obtained from participating department chairmen and deans, funding was approved, and a development team was organized. The library was represented by the author, the English department by Blaine Hall (who holds master's degrees in both English and library science), and the University's Instructional Development Program by Dr. Irwin Goodman, whose office funded the programs and directed the efforts of instructional psychologists, script writers, and electronic recording engineers.

Procedures to this point are shown in Table II as the Project Initiation Phase. This is followed by the Analysis Phase where philosophy and behavioral objectives are determined. A flow chart illustrating the Analysis Phase is shown in Table III. The first two steps in the Analysis Phase are to examine the characteristics of the student body for whom the

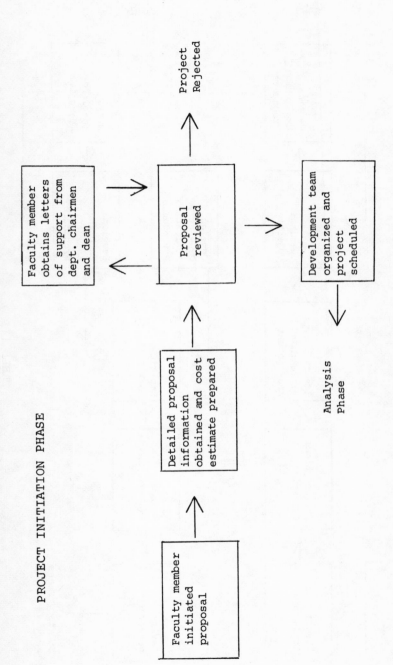

PROJECT INITIATION PHASE

Faculty member obtains letters of support from dept. chairmen and dean

Project Rejected

Proposal reviewed

Development team organized and project scheduled

Detailed proposal information obtained and cost estimate prepared

Analysis Phase

Faculty member initiated proposal

TABLE II

ANALYSIS PHASE

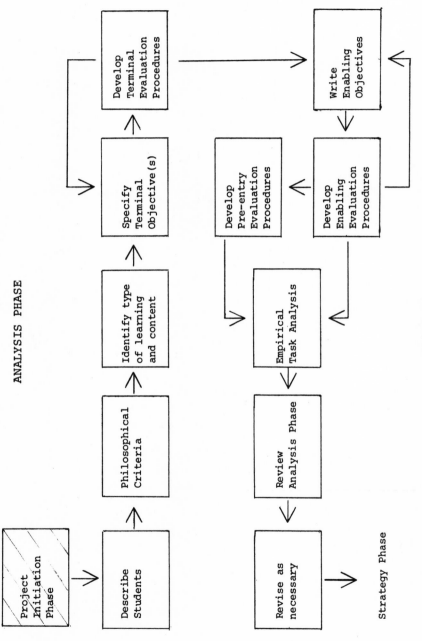

TABLE III

Strategy Phase

program is to be designed, and to develop the philosophical criteria for development.

For example, the Brigham Young University student body was examined and found to consist of freshman and sophomore students from all states of the union and from fifty-three foreign countries. They averaged 18-20 years of age, were 47% male and 53% female, and majored in most subject areas.

Several philosophical decisions were agreed upon:

Instruction would be written for the immediate needs of the student at the level of the curriculum for which he is enrolled. No effort would be made to teach all the student would ever need to know in any one year of his enrollment. This philosophy calls for instruction at all levels of the curriculum. The freshman would receive an orientation to physical facilities, the sophomore would receive basic instruction in the use of general library resources, and, in each year thereafter, the student would receive increasing levels of instruction in research techniques which directly pertain to his study in the curriculum.

Instruction would be designed to be administered within the library itself so that materials discussed would be in the hands of the patron. All instruction would be supplemented with assignments and tests also administered in the library. Computer scoring techniques would be utilized with test results being routed by the library to the student's instructor for teacher evaluation purposes.

An attempt would also be made to build in a high level of success while keeping costs of development to a minimum. Students need to feel that the time they spend is profitable and worthwhile. This is the primary reason for the use of an instructional psychology design.

27

Based upon such philosophical decisions, the Development Team decided to construct five instructional packages: a tape/cassette tour of physical facilities, instruction in the use of the card catalog, instruction in the use of periodical indexes, use of basic book and newspaper indexes, and use of basic U. S. government documents.

The card catalog program draws primarily from the expertise of the University's Department of Instructional Research and Development, a graduate educational psychology curriculum concerned with the development of instructional programs. Charles Bradshaw, a graduate assistant, was employed from that department to work on the development team with the assignment of formulating and testing behavioral objectives, designing the instructional package, and statistically validating the program. Mr. Bradshaw received direct supervision from Dr. M. David Merrill, chairman of that department. The content experts for the program were Mr. Hall, representing the English composition department, and the author, representing the library.

In developing the behavioral objectives for use of the card catalog, it was necessary to determine the types of learning involved. The thinking of Robert M. Gagne, a prominent instructional psychologist, was referred to in gaining insight to methods of learning. Dr. Gagne discussed eight types of learning in his book *The Conditions of Learning*.[4] They include:

Signal learning	Discrimination learning
Stimulus response	Concept learning
Chaining	Rule learning
Verbal association	Problem solving

Teaching skills in the use of library sources falls into the definition of concept learning. In order to learn concepts, one

28

must first memorize definitions (verbal association), then classify the definitions into concepts. After mastering several concepts, the student would be able to discriminate between several conceptional alternatives. For more detail on the application of Gagne's philosophy, it is strongly recommended that his book be read carefully.

The B. Y. U. instructional model calls for the formulation of terminal objectives which describe the kind of behavior a student would be expected to perform as a result of the instruction. The card catalog program has six "terminal objectives," gauged at the concept level of learning and describing six areas of card catalog use: 1) filing rules, 2) call numbers, 3) cross references, 4) author, title, and subject cards, 5) tracings, and 6) use of the book *Subject Headings Used in the Dictionary Catalogs of the Library of Congress*. A sample terminal objective on the use of "tracings" is listed in Figure 1.

Each objective is matched with a sample test question or questions that measure the performance of the objective. One of the test questions for the terminal objective on "tracings" is also illustrated in Figure 1.

In order to achieve the behavior called for in the instruction, it is helpful to write several supporting enabling objectives for each terminal objective. This is illustrated in Figure 2.

Three enabling objectives were written for the terminal objective on tracings. The student would be able to define "tracings," demonstrate where they are located on the card, and know that they can be used in three ways in research: 1) to determine the subjects assigned to a book, 2) to determine the kind of information contained in a book, and 3) to determine what added subject headings can be used to expand a bibliographical search.

29

BEHAVIORAL OBJECTIVE WORKSHEET

Identification Title: __*Terminal Objective on Tracings*__ No.: __5__

Project: ____*Card Catalog*_____ IDP No.: __005__

Type of Learning: _____*Concept Learning*_____

┌── Conditions (givens and restrictions): ──────────────────┐

*When given an author, title, or subject for which there is
a card in the card catalog*

└──┘

┌── Behavior ──┐

*The student will be able to determine additional related
subject headings to books of specific interest and use
those subject headings in an expanded search of a topic*

└──┘

┌── Criteria ──┐

100% accuracy in the 10 minutes

└──┘

Sample test items[5]

*The book War's Aftermath, by David Starr Jordan, has a lot of
information for which you are looking, but it is not enough.
What additional subject heading(s) could you best look under
to find more books related to this one?*

   a) Eugenics
   b) Balkan Peninsula - Hist. - War of 1912-1913
   c) Jordan, Harvey Ernest, 1878-
   d) European war, 1914-1918
   e) War-Macedonia

FIGURE 1

Instructional Development Program
Division of Instructional Services - Brigham Young University

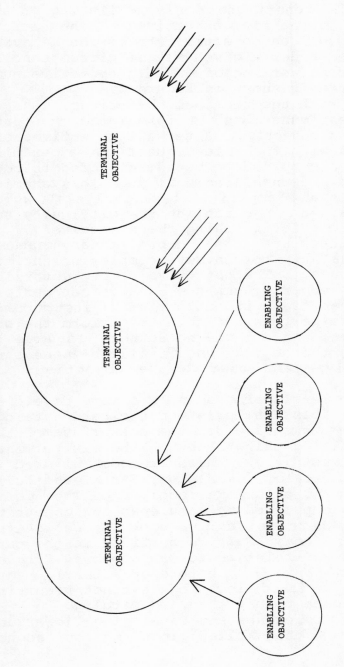

FIGURE 2

This constitutes only a listing of the kinds of enabling objectives. The actual wording of an objective states the behavior expected under a given set of circumstances. The formal wording of enabling objective number three is shown in Figure 3.

As with the terminal objectives, one or more test questions is formulated for each enabling objective. After all objectives are matched with their test questions, an examination is compiled to be administered to both skilled and unskilled subjects. This examination is an "empirical task analysis" which is designed to establish the difficulty and best order for teaching the objectives.

The task analysis is a preliminary measurement that does not involve complex scientific techniques. The objective is to determine if the experts and non-experts can perform the objectives without any prior instruction. If the expert is not able to perform the objectives, or if the non-expert is able to perform the objectives, it will be necessary to analyze and rewrite the objectives of concern.

Two levels of examination were developed for the "task analysis" on the card catalog:

Part One called for the actual use of the card catalog using each of the six terminal objectives (*e.g.*, Which are books listed in the card catalog *about*, not by, Sara Teasdale?)[6]

Part Two called for memory recall of definitions supported by each enabling objective (*e.g.*, Where would the book *21 Delightful Ways to Commit Suicide* be filed in the card catalog in relation to the book *20 Elegant Ways to Cook Eel*, before or after?)[7] Part Two is a fixed location test not requiring the student to use the card catalog.

Four reference and cataloging librarians served as the skilled group and four sopho-

BEHAVIORAL OBJECTIVE WORKSHEET

Identification Title: _Enabling Objective #3 on_   No.: _5_
                                     Tracings

Project: _Card Catalog_   IDP No.: _005_

Type of Learning: _Memorization_

Conditions (givens and restrictions):

_When given an author, title, or subject card used in
the card catalog_

Behavior

_The student will be able to understand that "tracings" can be
used to, a) determine the type of information found in the
book, b) know what subject(s) and added entries have been
assigned to the book, and c) tell what additional subject
headings could be consulted for information related to a
particular book._

Criteria

100% in 15 minutes

Sample test items

FIGURE 3

Instructional Development Program
Division of Instructional Services - Brigham Young University

more students served as the unskilled group. The librarians scored 98% correct on the test in 48 minutes while the students answered only 32% correct in 2-1/2 hours. Students were required to terminate their test after 2-1/2 hours. During the examination, half of the participants were observed from a distance for their reactions without comment by the observer. This observation was helpful in determining where the librarian or student was frustrated or confused. The remaining participants were observed at close range and were often asked for an explanation of both positive and negative reactions. In this way, a greal deal of early feedback was received to assist in the actual writing of the instruction.

The task analysis for the card catalog did confirm the selection of the objectives and their arrangement in an effective hierarchy. A few revisions were built into the objectives and test questions, and the pre- and post-tests to be used in the actual program were finalized from the task analysis. The test questions for Part Two of the task analysis were based upon enabling objectives, and became the pretest. The test questions to Part One made use of the actual card catalog, were based upon the terminal objectives, and became the posttest.

This completed the Analysis Phase of the program. Next came a Strategy Phase. A flow chart of this procedure is shown in Table IV. An instructional strategy was based upon the types of learning involved. It was mentioned earlier that the teaching of concepts (the most common level called for in teaching the use of libraries) involves the memorization of definitions (verbal association), and their classification into concepts. Part of the Strategy Phase is to select, in light of the

STRATEGY PHASE

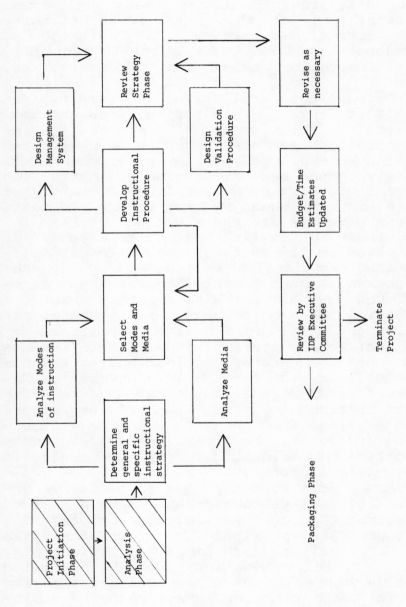

TABLE IV

types of learning involved, the formal means of presentation, *i.e.*, tutoring, laboratory, homework, individualized learning, etc. Another part of this phase is to determine what form of media to use, *i.e.*, textbooks, handbooks, slides, tapes, still pictures, oral instruction, television, motion pictures, etc.

Because the card catalog program involves 4,000 students a year and requires the mastery of a large number of concepts, the individualized learning approach was selected in the form of a textbook, or programmed text. This was done because programmed instruction is individualized and utilizes a mastery of each concept when continuing to the next. These concepts are thereby tied together until there is a unified body of knowledge. It involves small - step coverage with carefully defined behavioral objectives so that the student knows exactly where he is going. Programmed instruction also insists upon the modification of the program throughout development until a high level of performance is guaranteed. Its individualization permits students to take only the instruction that is needed. It also frees a large number of instructors from the many demands of teaching such vast numbers of students. If instructors can be freed from the details of the instruction, costs will be greatly reduced and the program will financially pay for itself, if not yield a profit.

Other techniques may be more effective under different circumstances. A hand-carried cassette tape unit was selected in designing a tour of the physical facilities within the 1,000,000 volume Clark Library. Bibliography and lecture combinations have been adopted for many upper-division and graduate programs where basic concepts have already been mastered and where the numbers of students involved were greatly reduced. Selection of a technique must be based upon the circumstances surrounding each program and its use.

The next step in the Strategy Phase was to develop the instructional procedure (see Table IV). To do so, management and validation procedures needed to be designed.

The management system deals with the physical means by which the program would be administered. Applied to the card catalog program, students purchase the programmed text, take the pretest, study the instructional material, and finally, take the departmental posttest in the library that is computer graded. The results of the departmental test would be routed by the library to the English instructor in whose class the student is enrolled. The details of this procedure comprise the management system.

The validation procedure involves the design of statistical validation techniques which prove the workability of the program. The University's Computer Science Department helped in setting up sample sizes, randomization processes, test procedures, and the analysis of the data. The validation procedure for the card catalog program is given in Figure 4.

Project: Card Catalog
Validation Procedure

	Pretest 1	Instruction	Pretest 2	Posttest
Experimental Group I Programmed Instruction	x	yes	x	x
Experimental Group II Nonprogrammed Instruction	x	yes	x	x
Control Group No Instruction	x	no	-	x

Figure 4

37

It was decided to make use of two experimental groups and one control group. The first experimental group receives the programmed instruction for which the package was originally designed. The second group receives a nonprogrammed version of the instruction for comparison purposes. The control group is given the pretest and posttest with no instruction. This would determine the amount of learning contained in the pretest instrument.

It was also decided to give an alternate form of the pretest (known as pretest 2) after giving instruction and before giving the posttest. (Remember that the pretest is a fixed-location test not requiring the student to use the actual card catalog.) If pretest 2 results are comparable to those in the posttest, it would indicate the feasibility of using a fixed-location test in place of the posttest in a published version of the program. This would permit other universities to make use of this program without being required to redesign the posttest to their specific card catalog.

At this point the Strategy Phase was reviewed and revised and the Packaging Phase begun. Packaging involved the final writing of the program and its assemblage into a usable product. An explanation of this phase is shown in Table V.

It is helpful to continually collect sample instructional materials already produced and to either make use of them as is, or adapt them to meet specific needs. These materials can also serve as guidelines for assembling original instructional materials.

Because behavioral objectives and the pre- and posttests were constructed during the Analysis Phase, instruction could easily be written to conform with those objectives and

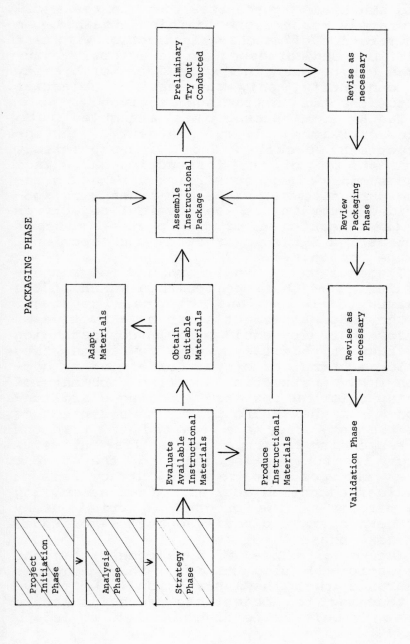

PACKAGING PHASE

Project Initiation Phase → Analysis Phase → Strategy Phase

Evaluate Available Instructional Materials

Obtain Suitable Materials

Adapt Materials

Produce Instructional Materials

Assemble Instructional Package

Preliminary Try Out Conducted

Revise as necessary

Review Packaging Phase

Revise as necessary

Validation Phase

TABLE V

test questions. Writing the instruction at this stage also guarantees that the tests will accurately measure the learning attained. An illustration of matching instruction with test questions and corresponding behavioral objectives can be seen in Figure 5. For brevity and continuity, only one enabling objective in the chapter on tracings is given.

The B. Y. U. package was assembled into three divisions: 1) the pretest, 2) the instructional package, and 3) the posttest. Each section of the instruction had a last page summary of concepts for review and stepping purposes. All three divisions were subdivided according to the terminal objectives so that section 1 of the pretest matched section 1 of the instruction and section 1 of the posttest.

Students score their own pretest and determine from their performance which of the instructional sections they need to study. If they have a perfect score on a section of the pretest, they could omit the corresponding instruction. If they miss a few items, they could go to the end of the corresponding section in the instruction and find a summary of concepts for the few items needing clarification. If they score poorly on a section of the pretest, they are advised to take the corresponding instruction in its entirety. After instruction is completed, the student takes the posttest to find out how well he has learned the objectives. After assembling the materials, the program is tried out by the developers and reviewed before moving to the next phase.

The final phase of development was the validation of the program. This provides assurance that the instruction is effective in teaching the objectives and helps locate any difficulties needing further revision.

40

CARD CATALOG

Enabling Objectives

When given an author, title, or subject card used in the card catalog, the student will be able to understand that "tracings" can be used to...tell what additional subject headings could be consulted for information related to a particular book

Test Question

The Arabic numeral(s) in the tracings on a library card,
a) indicate additional *book* titles available and related to this one,
b) indicate title and/or author cards available on that particular book,
c) both a & b
d) indicate related subject heading cards available
e) I'm not sure

Instruction

Suppose you wanted to do a paper on the subject "Local Church Councils." You would first look up that heading in the card catalog and you might find only one book on the subject *Church cooperation in the United States*. If you didn't know how to use tracings, you would be limited to that one book.

Question 5

With your knowledge of tracings, the listing on the card in Figure 5 refers you to how many other subject headings?

Answer

Two additional subject headings

If you were to look up the other two subject headings you might find that "interdenominational cooperation" has six books under its heading and that "Christian union history" has an additional eleven books under its heading.

FIGURE 5[8]

The steps of validation are given in Table VI. Inasmuch as B. Y. U. students signed up for English composition courses by section number, and most sections are listed as being taught by "staff" it was felt by the development team that a random sample for field testing was easily available by taking 161 sophomore English students from three sections. All students were randomly divided into three groups: 1) Group I (73 students) receiving the cassette tape of programmed instruction, 2) Group II (51 students) receiving the non-programmed version, and 3) Group III (50 students) serving as a control group and receiving no instruction.

All groups were given pretest 1 in their respective classrooms. Students in Groups I and II determined from the results of their pretest scores which areas of instruction they should study. They were also aware that they would receive a posttest which would evaluate how well they learned the information expected of them. Group I took the programmed instruction and Group II received the nonprogrammed version. Groups I and II were then given pretest 2. (Remember, the two pretests were fixed-location tests.) All groups then took the posttest. A summary of the results are given in Figure 6.

MEAN SCORES

	Pretest 1 (29 ques.)	Instruction yes/no	Pretest 2 (29 ques.)	Posttest (26 ques.)
Group I (n = 73) Programmed Instruction	9.8	yes	22.4	21.5
Group II (n = 51) Nonprogrammed Instruction	9.5	yes	19.2	18.6
Group III (n = 50) Control	9.0	no	--	12.7

FIGURE 6[9]

42

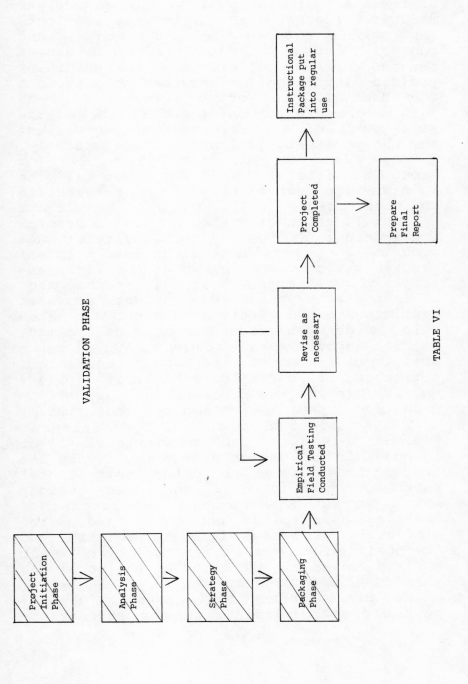

VALIDATION PHASE

Project Initiation Phase → Analysis Phase → Strategy Phase → Packaging Phase → Empirical Field Testing Conducted → Revise as necessary → Project Completed → Instructional Package put into regular use

Project Completed → Prepare Final Report

TABLE VI

Using the Scheffe and Least Significance Difference Test an analysis of covariance was made with pretest 1 as the covariate. Posttest scores between the experimental and control groups (18.6 and 12.7) and between the two experimental groups (21.5 and 18.6) yielded significant differences both at less than the .01 level of significance. Mean gain scores for Groups I and II showed the same level of significance between pretest and the posttest, 11.7 and 9.1 respectively. This was an increase from 32% to 84% for Group I and from 32% to 72% for Group II. The gain of the control group from pretest 1 to the posttest (9.0 to 12.7) was nonsignificant.

The validation of a program yields several implications as to the workability of that program. It is possible that an instructional program may be found invalid at the first attempt of validation. If this is the case, it is necessary to analyze the data and test participants and determine the reasons. When this is done, necessary changes can be made to bring about the validity and intended workability of a program. If such procedures are not taken, it is very possible that an ineffective program would be put into use, often resulting in poor motivation and confusion.

The validation of the B. Y. U. program yielded three important conclusions: 1) it is possible to design effective library use instructional materials using instructional psychology techniques, 2) there was a slight but important advantage to the programmed learning approach in the study, and 3) the similarity of scores between pretest 2 and the posttest suggest the feasibility of using a fixed location posttest for the published version of the program.

The Clark Library still uses the departmental posttest requiring the student to locate his answers in the card catalog. It is felt that there is a reinforcement motivation in actually using the card catalog in locating the cards called for. The departmental posttest also permits us to continually evaluate the program through computer scoring and analysis. The computer scored tests can then be routed to the student's instructor, thus freeing him from designing a test for his evaluation purposes.

It is necessary to continually evaluate developed programs in respect to the objectives they are designed to accomplish. Prerequisites, library systems, and people do change. When the time comes that good things cannot be made better, librarians can retire.

The procedures presented in this paper draw upon established principles of instructional psychology, and, if followed properly, will work. They are not the answer to all problems in library use instruction, but they are important if one desires to build a program that will contain built-in guarantees of reaching specific behavioral objectives.

The illustration of the card catalog program was intended to serve as a concrete guide or practical application of the model. As the "Sea Horse, cantering out to find his fortune," I do hope we as librarians will be sure to first determine where we are going and then proceed in that direction.

Notes

1. Robert F. Mager, *Preparing Objectives for Programmed Instruction*, (San Francisco: Fearon Publishers, 1962), p. ix.
2. Dr. R. Irwin Goodman, Director of the Brigham Young University Instructional Development Program in conjunction with Dr. M. David Merrill, Chairman of the Brigham

45

Young University Department of Research and Development devised the philosophical model from which this program was developed. Tables I through VI are adapted from models prepared by the Instructional Development Program, Division of Instructional Services, B. Y. U.

3. The author is indebted to Millicent Palmer, Library Instruction Librarian, Southern Illinois University Library at Edwardsville, Illinois, for her theoretical influence on the B. Y. U. program.
4. Robert M. Gagne, *The Conditions of Learning* (2nd ed.), (New York: Holt, 1970).
5. Reproduced from an unpublished departmental posttest on the card catalog in use at B. Y. U.
6. Charles I. Bradshaw with Marvin E. Wiggins and Blaine Hall, *Using the Library; the Card Catalog*, (Provo, Utah: B.Y.U. University Press, 1971), pp. 78-80.
7. *Ibid.*
8. *Ibid.*
9. Unpublished data provided by Charles I. Bradshaw and submitted to the Department of Instructional Research and Development, B. Y. U.

COMPUTER ASSISTED INSTRUCTION IN USE OF THE LIBRARY: ONE SOLUTION FOR THE LARGE UNIVERSITY

Alice S. Clark
The Ohio State University

A continual replication of published studies and our own statistics have convinced us that all too often undergraduate students in libraries are seeking a quiet study hall rather than an information center or a research facility. Billy R. Wilkinson has said, "All undergraduate libraries have been a screaming success as study halls" and has quoted studies at Michigan showing that 40 - 65 percent of students in the library are studying their own materials.[1] Still librarians cannot accept the idea that these facts absolve them from the responsibility to teach students the use of the library. This past year a flurry of activity on the subject of library instruction indicated that librarians were preoccupied with the problem, or at least there was a consensus of opinion that it really was a problem.

Looking over the literature that has been produced, especially the excellent state of the art report in the *Drexel Quarterly*,[2] and reviewing the various meetings, two conclusions seem to appear: 1) that library orientation and instruction programs must be adapted to

the size of the student body involved and 2)
that many kinds of teaching methods should be
employed to reach a varied community of students at varied levels of competency.

Several meetings have foundered on this
question of size. A lack of communication
occurs. Some very fine programs have been
developed in small institutions but the program for one thousand freshmen has little
direct carry over to the university with ten
thousand freshmen. However, the second conclusion that all kinds of teaching methods
must be used in any one institution brings us
back to a common ground. Some of our specific
teaching techniques can be applied in many
institutions. A good slide-tape presentation
on the use of indexes is a valuable tool any-
where. The best programs seem to combine a
number of different plans adapted to the vary-
ing needs of different students. Thus any
institution attempting to prepare a program
for library instruction can select bits and
pieces from the programs of other libraries.
We really do need to share our ideas at conferences like this one.

Probably we should deliberately avoid coming
to any conclusions about which programs are
most effective until the many research projects
now going on begin to approach the termination
of their experimental phases. We should all
consider ourselves to be in a research stage,
until we see the results of these programs
that have been funded by the Council on Library Resources and the National Endowment
for the Humanities.

A primary assumption in attacking the problem is this realization that no one program
is the answer. Rather it is what Thelma Larson
advised. She said, "Total involvement for the
four years is the ideal for which to strive."[3]
A multiplicity of experiences occurring during

his four year college career should provide the student with the knowledge sufficient for his own needs.

Large university libraries do have special problems. Roger Horn, in his recent article, "Think Big: The Evolution of Bureaucracy," described the transition of the college library committed to serving its user's needs to the university or research library which seems to exist for its own sake. He called our towers of book stacks monuments to the dead book -- dead in the sense that it is buried.[4]

Patricia Knapp also described the phenomenon when she said, "The university library system is quite naturally and inevitably responsive primarily to the library requirements of the graduate and research programs of the university"[5] and she saw the undergraduate library as the teaching instrument for approaching the system.

Large university libraries develop institutional distortions which seem designed to defeat the incoming freshmen. Sheer size and volume of traffic have brought about the need for closed stacks. While they may be necessary, they immediately distort our purpose by keeping the student away from the book. One of the saddest experiences we have is the young student who sidles up and says, "This is a stupid question, but where are the books?" This problem has been partially solved by building undergraduate libraries which have reduced the traffic in the research libraries and allowed the undergraduate his share of attention.

Another distortion sometimes occurs when libraries are suffering from space problems. Administrators may adopt temporary measures to increase study stations. This sometimes means assigning to the library's control classroom space adjoining the library or in nearby buildings, furnishing them with carrels as additional library seating. When we accept this solution we immediately lose one of our chief motivational methods which is to surround the studying student with supplemental materials and services which hopefully he will be attracted to use. These so-called "temporary measures" prevent our socialization of the student toward the use of libraries.

Another distortion is the too rigid specialization which makes our technical services librarians subsidiary to a numbers game of production. The bibliographer or cataloger who is working at the catalog is an obvious target for student inquiries. All too often these inquiries are shunted aside or brushde off. This isn't always because the librarian objects to doing public service and helping the student. Often this librarian welcomes the opportunity to see what the patron needs in the catalog and how the patron uses it. When the cataloger or bibliographer fails to take time to serve the student, it is often because our demands for production in technical services have forced him to think in terms of time study rather than in terms of people. But the student patron may be turned off from librarians for the rest of his college career.

Another institutional pressure arises through the constant demand from outside groups to visit the library. University libraries are exciting places. We do have fancy electronic carrels, computer projects and fine rare book rooms which people want to see. The constant requests for tours plagues university research libraries and those with new buildings especially, but all libraries suffer from it to a certain extent. At O.S.U. we have been forced to place limitations on tours so that our students can have the priority. We have a new and unique on-line circulation system, parti-

50

cipate in the O. C. L. C. cooperative system of cataloging from MARC tapes and have a new undergraduate learning resources center. Visitors quite understandably want to see these various kinds of computer terminals in action or see our carrels with video monitors and dial access facilities. We found this created two problems -- one, a constant disruption to people studying and two, a drain on our overworked personnel to provide demonstrations.

Our new tour policy spreads orientation tours so that there is no constant stream of noisy groups going by study areas. Tours to outsiders must be scheduled in advance and are limited to certain days. In this way we control the amount of disruption. We have already had one institute to demonstrate our circulation system and will conduct others. The fee charged for these institutes will compensate for the time our personnel will expend instructing these outsiders. Commercial firms who are using our facilities to demonstrate for their future customers in order to make sales of similar equipment will be charged a fee. This will allow us to add personnel to use for tour and demonstration purposes.

We have now gone on record that our priorities for tours and demonstrations will be: 1) our own students, 2) the rest of our campus community, 3) Ohio libraries and library schools (We are state supported.), 4) libraries and library schools outside of Ohio (We do recognize our obligation to the profession), 5) paid tours for commercial firms and 6) others.

This "others" group is a difficult one since our university public relations office runs bus tours around the campus and has been known to bring forty or fifty elementary school children, club groups, and senior citizen groups unannounced for a tour of the building. We have had to explain that students studying

51

in the library should not be disturbed any more than students in classrooms. We must be careful that we are not offering better orientation to strangers than to our own students.

Another distortion occurs when library orientation and instruction are thought of as strictly an undergraduate library function rather than as a concern of the whole library staff. Teaching the use of the library has been a traditional function of the academic library and as such is the responsibility of the whole library organization rather than a distinctive task assigned to an orientation librarian or even to the undergraduate libraries as a department.

In our efforts to get faculty status in academic libraries we have always stressed that we do teach in the library. Usually this is on an individual basis. It is what we have always done and what we do best. While the cooperation of the teaching faculty is important, teaching library use is a library responsibility. Undoubtedly there is a carry-over factor from department to department of the college or university and each subject field may help to motivate students to learn more about another field. This carry-over is important between the library and other departments but the responsibility for our motivation and instruction still lies with us in the library.

We are one of the few faculties in the university system who must teach without the motivational force of the grading system. We know therefore that we have to find unusual ways to motivate our students. We have to take full advantage of theories on socialization and motivation. We already knew this empirically since when we built attractive new buildings or added carpeting, circulation increased. While motivation problems seem more severe to us, we have been fortunate in having what other teaching faculty desire--the freedom from grades and the directive to teach individually -- the independent study route which other departments are just beginning to achieve. Rather than attempt to adapt our teaching to the stereotyped lecture that students find irrelevant, perhaps we need to recognize that for years we have been lucky enough to be leaders toward teaching a student to study what he wants when he wants it. Perhaps we need to concentrate any special programs on creating the opportunity where more of this one-to-one instruction can take place. The orientation librarian and the undergraduate librarian have the duty to acquaint the student with services that are available and to introduce him to the areas where this one-to-one instruction can be given.

But beyond this basic orientation the student deserves our best -- those same services he has always received but in greater quantity to more students. Our best is the expert librarian teaching the individual student at the time that he has need for the instruction. We are not the only department on campus guilty of forgetting this people -to- people contact. Many departments become overloaded with administrators and researchers to the neglect of good teaching. Many have made the mistake of putting teaching in the hands of teaching assistants and lecturers while the full professor never sees more than a few graduate advisees.

Some of the experimental orientation programs have begun to use students as reference aides based on the fact that students are less reluctant to ask questions of their peers. This is a good approach step but the student aide like the teaching assistant is not the dedicated careerist that the professional librarian is. He can't be taught in the few years he is on campus to know very much about library research. At Ohio State we use student assistants for undergraduate library reference especially in late evening hours and on weekends. Even here we find quite a long time is needed just to teach our student assistants where various services are located so that they can properly direct patrons. (Is horticulture in the Agriculture Library or in the Botany Library? Where is biophysics?) Some of our student assistants become quite expert at basic tools but they often need to rely heavily upon an extensive vertical file and on our mimeographed bibliographies and guides. At best this is only an approach step.

In a real reference situation, like a university library reference room, even beginning librarians are of little use. There is a good reason why advertisements for university reference librarians usually specify previous experience and here again usually *university* reference experience. Even the senior reference librarians, our elite who become expert at using a reference collection of 60,000 volumes, still aren't expected to give in-depth service in a subject field and refer many researchers to a department librarian.

We have also tried using library assistants at the catalog information desk and have reverted to using librarians. All too often what appeared to be a catalog-use question really turned out to be a request for instruction in how to do a subject search.

Herein too lies the danger when all library instruction is left to orientation and undergraduate librarians. We have been forced to realize that the undergraduate library can't do the whole teaching job. A request for lectures in the bibliography of industrial design for sophomore level courses eventually had to be referred to the graduate research consultant. The field required expertise in materials that appeared in the Engineering Library, the Commerce Library, the Education Library where much of the psychology collection is kept, and in the Fine Arts Library. The research consultant, a full professor, was able to pull these materials together and reduce the approach to an undergraduate level. Her lectures were supplemented by tours of the main reference room given by reference librarians who attended the lectures and who pointed out some of the sources located there. This type of instruction may be too expensive to offer to every sophomore but it should be available when the class needs it.

As in this case, we do sometimes need to use classroom instruction. There is a reluctance on the part of some librarians to do group teaching. While to a certain extent we can schedule around this, we need to encourage librarians to feel teaching is a part of librarianship. Library schools must be made to recognize this so that people do not enter the profession under a misapprehension. While the profession needs the scholarly, book-oriented bibliographer, in an academic situation he must also be willing to share his expertise not only with the teaching faculty but also with students. When the student activists criticize the research professor who won't teach classes they are really also criticizing the unavailable librarian. If we have had fewer attacks from students it is only because we have kept the scholarly librarian well hidden.

However, once we accept the fact that instruction is a function of the total library staff, we find that usually the individual approach is best. There are really two reasons for this. One is, of course, that the student moves along at his own pace from level to level of need. Martha Hackman's model for library instruction is based on a philosophy of division on this basis of levels of need. She recommended a varied program allowing the student to enter at the level of his current requirements.[6]   Some of our lack of communication at the meetings on library orientation has occurred because we were talking about many different levels and depths of instruction. In a university situation several levels can be determined, including orientation with the objective of removing fear and bringing the non-user inside the building; basic instruction in use of the card catalog, indexes, basic reference tools and special services available; instruction in sources of a major field; and in-depth subject bibliography.

The other reason for the individual approach is the difference in students' life goals and career objectives which produces many different kinds of information needs.   We should recognize that some students will be corporate executives whose research is done for them by a special librarian or information scientist on a total service basis. He will never leave his desk for information service, and our duty to him may be to acquaint him with this concept of total service. In some area of the library system he should be provided with service which prepares pre-packaged information--perhaps in an expanded vertical file.   In our system at O.S.U. it may mean introducing him to the Mechanized Information Center which provides current awareness service by computer search of several data bases.

We also have a duty to turn students into regular public library users.   This may be primarily a socialization to the feeling that libraries are pleasant places to use. We may be serving his needs best by emphasizing our current reading rooms, fiction collections and providing him with pleasant surroundings. However, we need to be sure he knows that librarians are there to help him when he has an information problem. We would not want the future housewife to see her public library only as a source of recreational reading. We also want her to seek out the reference librarian when she is doing a project for the League of Women Voters.

Undoubtedly most of our resources will be devoted to those students wanting to know how to do their own research. Their needs may range from a few basic reference books to advanced bibliography. This student needs to be encouraged to move from level to level. If he reaches a level at his senior year that is comparable to the doctoral candidate's, he should receive the same services and instruction. At this level he may be working with a senior reference librarian as a team jointly discovering bibliographic sources.

In a large institution financial restrictions make it necessary that we concentrate on filling the student's needs as they arise rather than to attempt blanket instruction at a time when he is not motivated to learn. We need to avoid the forced library lecture--what Patricia Knapp called the "technical high-schoolish programs."[7] She recommended self-teaching devices for those needing basic instruction.

This concept does seem to be spreading among larger university libraries. Iowa State, which has had a good orientation program with a five-week non-credit course and a ten-week one-credit course taught to five thousand students, has recently put the uniform parts of these courses on cassette tapes with an accompanying folder of materials. This permits individual make-up of classes missed and independent study for honors groups, and frees instructors for more individual conferences.[8]

At The Ohio State University Libraries we have been adopting computer assisted instruction as a technique for providing this type of individual instruction. Our objective in developing CAI courses is to present short modules of information for orientation rather than in-depth instruction. We are trying to familiarize the students with some of the problems of library use, to remove any fear he may have about showing his ignorance and to help him formulate the questions he should ask the library staff which will lead him into the ideal one-to-one instruction by experts which we feel we should provide.

Our choice of CAI as a technique is based on similar individual approaches used elsewhere. Paul Wendt used programmed instruction in teaching machines to give individual instruction at Southern Illinois University.[9] Marina E. Axeen developed a complete course using CAI at the University of Illinois.[10] CAI modules using a CRT terminal are being developed at the University of Denver. The Model Library which is part of the INTREX program at Massachusetts Institute of Technology has developed point-of-use instruction by providing dial access audio or audio-visual instruction. For example they have a tape and slide presentation next to the *Science Citation Index* explaining the tool and its use.

These brief individual presentations using modern technology may be either orientation or instruction. They provide a wider availability than we can provide with staff teaching for they work nights and week-ends and don't take lunch hours. They are impersonal and students need to have no fear of showing their ignorance to a machine. We are developint the CAI course in modules each limited to the specific information problem which the student has at a given time. His motivation comes from his own need.

Our primary audience is the freshmen but a secondary audience could be anyone with the need for orientation. Several ways will be used to alert students to the availability of the courses. Notices will be posted at appropriate points in the libraries including the CAI terminal area. Announcements will be made on orientation tours and at library lectures. Since our orientation program is integrated with the university one-credit orientation course, UVC 100, and with the study techniques course, Psychology 120, these students will also be alerted. As new modules are added, announcements will be placed in the campus daily newspaper.

Each of the modules of instruction will be about one half hour long. At present we plan to have one on the use of the catalog, one on reading LC call numbers and locating books on the shelf, one providing some information about department libraries, one on finding book reviews, one on use of indexes, and an introduction to some basic reference tools. Each module will be accompanied by additional materials appropriate to its content. The student taking the catalog-use course will check out an actual drawer of cards. The programmed instruction requires that he actually look up a card and type some bit of information from it back into the computer terminal. The department libraries sequence will include slides showing some scenes both outside and inside the buildings. The index sequence will use actual sample indexes for the instruction.

The structure of the courses will be based on student interaction, a dialog with the computer. Brief instruction statements are followed by practice in doing some action or feed-back to prove comprehension.

CAI terminals are located in both undergraduate libraries for use in all CAI courses. Most of these are IBM 2741 typewriter terminals but Novar 541 or NCR 260 are also used. Our CAI system has 26 ports plus 2 supervisory ports and uses the same computer as our library circulation system, an IBM 360/50 which will soon be replaced with a larger system. The terminals in the libraries are encased in a carrel designed to be used in quiet areas. These carrels, which were designed at Ohio State, include work space and built-in projector and screen space to integrate audio-visual media with CAI.

Preparation of the modules is very time-consuming. Robert Strum and John Ward in "Some Comments on Computer Assisted Instruction in Engineering Education" have listed some of the disadvantages including "the immense effort required to prepare course material for the system" and "the high cost of hardware and program preparation."[11] Our CAI division has identified the developmental phases as follows:

Identifying the personnel
Suitability of material to CAI
Design of a module
Entry of data
Completion of one module
Debugging
Testing
Making changes based on use
Making the module available for use
Completion of other modules

Our first module is in the testing stage. This is extremely important since CAI permits open ended questions and the system must interpret the answers as right or wrong. This means every possible option must be identified and added to the program.

This short course, which is designed as orientation rather than instruction, provides an introduction to the use of the card catalog. Its purpose is to point out some of the complications that occur in catalog filing, to encourage the student to be more persistent in searching for the correct card and to furnish him with enough knowledge so that he will have no fear about asking for help. Several concepts are presented: letter by letter and word by word filing, elimination of initial articles, various entries used, content of the cards, dictionary and divided catalogs, the subject heading list, subject arrangements (person, place and thing), punctuation and chronological arrangements. Some of these may be eliminated and other concepts added as a result of the current testing on students.

As yet no plans have been made to compare the knowledge of students using the CAI courses with any control groups. Axeen's study which compared the CAI instruction with a control group getting conventional lectures showed "The experimental and control group did not differ significantly in the amount of knowledge gained..."[12]

Regardless of its measure of success, it can be regarded only as one more approach to be used in a complex system of methods for total library instruction.

Notes

1. Billy R. Wilkinson, "A Screaming Success as Study Halls," *Library Journal*, 96 (May 1, 1971), p. 1567.
2. *Drexel Library Quarterly* 7 (July & October, 1971).
3. Thelma Larson, "The Public Onslaught: a Survey of User Orientation Methods," *RQ*, 8 (Spring, 1969), p. 188.

4. Roger Horn, "Think Big: The Evolution of Bureaucracy," *College and Research Libraries*, 33 (January, 1972), p. 17.
5. Patricia B. Knapp, "Guidelines for Bucking the System: A Strategy for Moving Toward the Ideal of the Undergraduate Library as a Teaching Instrument," *Drexel Library Quarterly*, 7 (July & October, 1971), p. 220.
6. Martha Hackman, "Proposal for a Program of Library Instruction," *Drexel Library Quarterly*, 7 (July & October, 1971), pp. 299-308.
7. Knapp, *op. cit.*, p. 218.
8. Iowa State University Library, *Annual Report, 1970-71*, pp. 21-22.
9. Paul Wendt, "Programmed Instruction for Transfer to the Real Life Situation," In *Proceedings of the National Conference on the Implications of the New Media for the Teaching of Library Science*. (Urbana: University of Illinois, 1963), pp. 77-79.
10. Marina E. Axeen, *Teaching the Use of the Library to Undergraduates: an Experimental Comparison of Computer-Based Instruction and the Conventional Lecture Method*. (Urbana: University of Illinois, 1967).
11. Robert Strum and John Ward, "Some Comments on Computer Assisted Instruction in Engineering Education," *IEEE Transactions on Education*, E-10 (March, 1967), pp. 1-3. Quoted by Swanson, Rowena W. *Move the Information: A Kind of Missionary Spirit*. (Arlington, Va.: Office of Aerospace Research, U.S. Air Force, 1967), p. 116.
12. Axeen, *op. cit.*, p. 74.

the physical things that we can "do" in a library; it is also a cabala, an essence we believe in and impart to others. This is the
virus which must infect students--the philosophy of a self-perpetuating liberal education.

To be operative--ready for use by students
--the library must be administratively sound
and philosophically envisioned. It must be
staffed with humanists alert and consenting
to the needs and problems of people, not just
the demands of accurate records. It must be
supplied with media other than print as well
as print, because learning comes not only from
reading, but as importantly from viewing, "gut"
feeling, and touching. Then, to be truly ready
for action, the balance of *people* resources
and *media* resources must be completely accessible. Such a library is ecologically stable,
a balanced economy. Achieving this philosophy
of operation is the first step toward involving students in library orientation projects.

The second step toward involving students
in orientation projects is to make them *aware*
of the library. The usual ways of developing
awareness of the library have been tours or
lectures in English classes or scurrying to
other classes with a cart full of books in
order to present a well - prepared, neatly-
documented *tour de force*. As with all captive
audiences, the student so burdened respond
poorly. The experience may be expedient for the
librarian--but it is not organic for the students. It leaves the library outside of them--
not part of them. We are ready; they aren't.
What does this mean for us?

I think the awareness we seek to instill
in students must never be linked with any kind
of instruction. We have made a mistake to
confuse the issues. The one is a response to
the other. Learning *follows* knowing that one

65

wants to learn. Showing students around the library or lecturing to them about books that are in the library will not hook them intellectually and mold them into being library users. The tours and the *tours de force* of the past have not reached students.

The job ahead of us, that of engineering awareness, can take many forms. I think it is a situation thing -- it depends on you, the psychology of your group and your library. As in the play *Anna and the King of Siam*, it is a matter of "Getting to Know You." It calls for public relations, inside and outside the library.

At your seats there are papers provided so that each of you might write down ways you've used to promote an interest in and awareness of the library. Let's now share your ideas alternately with samples I bring you from Wabash. Here's one to start: freshmen entering Wabash first meet the library with their parents in late August at the President's reception for them in its air-conditioned setting. Self-guided tours are distributed. There are no conducted tours, but there are students stationed throughout the library ready to answer questions. These student guides are already involved in the library, in the programs being instituted through our matching grant from the Council on Library Resources, soon to be discussed.

Now would someone here give us an awareness idea from another library? Please identify yourself and your library first.

Participation from Group

Another idea from Wabash. Each spring, top-ranking students from high schools in the midwest visit Wabash for a weekend of examinations and exposure to the campus. Over 300

66

of these "honors" scholars swarm into the library on a late Friday afternoon for punch, chips, dip and rapping before their evening program. Faculty are invited. And, again, students who have "experienced" the library act as hosts and interpret the library to the visitors.

Participation

"Little environments" -- original creative displays advertising the library are constructed by students involved in the living unit program. Euripides Tsakarides, an especially artistic student in the seminar program, selected a display as a project to work on between encounters at the Reference Desk. He advised and assisted in the making of these "environments" in cooperating dormitories and fraternities.

This spring, Euripides has had charge of a feed-back bulletin board in the library on which paper and pencils are provided with a weekly question for students to respond to -- an opportunity to gauge their feelings and reactions to questions such as "What is a library?" and "What can a library be?" The idea for mechanism of feedback was his.

Participation

Reaching out, the library provides records which the campus radio station uses for much of the musical broadcasts.

To keep the library in focus in the weekly student newspaper, regular news items are forwarded to the editor of the student newspaper from members of the library staff.

Participation

The Reference Librarian makes herself available to the living unit, on invitation, for after-dinner conversation about the library. A number of fraternities have had her as dinner guest prior to this library dialog -- a sharing, not a teaching.

Having the staff get out of the library is a way of involving students in the library. If a librarian can have dinner or coffee and doughnuts with students and faculty, can meet on an informal person-to-person basis, a contact is made. The students and faculty begin to feel that they have someone to go to for help in the library. The librarian seen at a student production, viewing an exhibition, or attending a lecture establishes rapport for the library and a sense of the library's part in the college community. Too frequently librarians have not acted as members of the group. With the host of other obstacles, it is not to be wondered that many have not been accepted as academic peers.

Participation

Students become involved in the library in direct proportion to faculty involvement in the library. Course-related help is the ideal, but can we wait forever to be asked? A little selective dissemination of information -- a telephone call or a note recommending an article, recording or new book--may go a long way toward making the professor aware of the help available in the library for him and his students. But why wait for a question? Make a contact creatively, aggressively. Even ask for help with a problem! Do something to break the ice.

All of the activities we have outlined are
samples of seeds that sprout the harvest of
greater library use. But this is not yet the
harvest. Students will not become involved
unless the library tells them what it is.
Albert Camus could very well have been speak-
ing about a library when he wrote movingly of
man's predicament in a sick society:

If a man wants to be recognized, he must
simple say who he is. If he is silent
or lies, he will die alone, and everything around him will be condemned to
disaster. But if he speaks the truth,
he will die undoubtedly, but after having
helped others and himself to live.[4]

Like man, the library must have an identity,
an integrity.

Libraries are being questioned today for
their relevance, usefulness, and cost. The
passive library and the passive librarian are
doomed. It's either time to go tell it on
the mountain--or die.

So the second step in involving students
in library orientation projects is making them
aware of the existence and potential of the
library.

The third step is the most challenging part
of orientation today -- that of designing experiences for students which will involve them
in the use of the library. And it is seriously
a matter of designing experiences rather than
dispensing information.

In its 14th Annual Report, the Council on
Library Resources spelled out a need which I
think those of us involved in library orientation have not reckoned into our programs
nearly enough: "active cooperation among the
principals." Let me quote from that report:

More than ever our society needs thought-
ful men and women with a sense of history,

69

to protect the democratic institutions
that merit it and reconstruct those that
require it. The libraries of our col-
leges and universities are central to
the educational process that can and must
produce the reservoir of national leadership to take us safely through the
decades ahead... The academic library's
function goes well beyond mere support
for the teaching program. It has the
potential to sharpen a student's intellectual curiosities to the point where
they will demand satisfaction all his
life. It must use that potential and
apply its resources to make itself the
full partner in the education of the
student. As in any partnership, active
cooperation among the principals is a
sine qua non.[5]

"Active cooperation" of all students in the
process of learning about the library is our
cabala at Wabash -- our black stone and our
North Star. I don't have any answers for you
or blueprints. I can only suggest possibilities with which I am familiar. Like Conant,
we're still exploring the problem from different approaches and our path next year will
no doubt be different from this year's.

Why? Because change, or experimentation,
produces waste products. As waste accumulates,
we must modify our work to reduce the amount
of slag. The waste products I am concerned
about -- and this would make another paper --
can largely be tabulated in the following
categories:

1. *Inefficiency.* Engendered when too few
   people work on too large a problem with
   too little help. Sound familiar?
2. *Communication failure.* *"Mea culpa,"* we
   say, too late. "I knew this. Why didn't
   everybody else?

70

3. *Insecurity*. Change is bound to rock somebody's boat, and visible or invisible resistance will inevitably result.
4. *The unreached*. Working with models, one still longs to reach all and is haunted by those unreached—"the great unwashed," as intern Mike Wilson so graphically puts it.

With these concerns, I still take heart from a favorite quotation from Michael Polayni's *The Tacit Dimension:*

It is the image of humanity immersed in potential thought that I find revealing for the problems of our day. It rids us of the absurdity of absolute self-determination, yet offers each of us the chance of creative originality, within the fragmentary area which circumscribes our calling. It provides us with the metaphysical grounds and the organizing principle of a Society of Explorers.[6]

I think that's what we are in higher education today -- a society of explorers -- with no one exploring more than the librarian whose multi-media world is a many-splendored thing. *And* a Pandora's box. Full of slag! and many bugs.

The failures and the waste make it vitally necessary to have the Polanyis and the Hentoffs and the Maslows giving direction and encouragement. They're all in our libraries--our consultants on an informal, nondirective basis, keeping us on course, helping us to clarify our goals.

In addition to the instruction which takes place in every reference encounter in the Wabash Library, there are as noted earlier, two ongoing programs which involve students in the library.

The freshman seminar program was initiated in September, 1970, the first of the programs to operate under a matching grant from the Council on Library Resources. In this program, professors who have a particular interest area outside of the usual curriculum offer a course in it, on an elective basis, to members of the freshman class. There have been seminars on "Censorship," "The Literature of World War I," "Linguistics," "Applied Genetics," and others.

Assisting each professor is a senior or upperclassman selected because of his scholarship and interest in the topic. He helps organize the class, plan the course of study, and conduct meetings. He also acts as the bibliographic consultant for the group--having participated in a library workshop before the semester began. The workshop is non-structured, problem-centered, and open to the faculty as well as the students involved.

It is presumed that all involved in the seminar--professor, student assistant, and the students attending -- are highly motivated . Students enroll in the seminar as an elective, which implies a degree of interest. This interest presumably will motivate them to use the library to develop their knowledge.

This spring we began another program -- one for in-house reference assistants. These students, on completion of eight 90 - minute learning sessions, act as library consultants to fellow students in the living units. The program was initiated after spring vacation, when students are beginning the long stretch toward finals, with many papers due within about six weeks.

A number of students volunteered for the project, and from these volunteers one representative was elected from each library unit. These students who already have an awareness of the library, are interested in learning, as well as in helping others develop an awareness of learning resources in others. All have outgoing personalities, and are interested in "becoming."

Motivation of students is extremely important in library orientation. Along with many other problems in our depressed 70's, we are faced with what Jerome Bruner in *The Relevance of Education* has termed "the new disengagement,"[7] an intellectual and political alienation. Unless students feel a need for instruction, they will drag their feet until we show what the library can do for them. And if they're in college less for education than for the union card that the degree has become, we really have a problem.

There are six basic tenets in the Wabash instructional programs, which although intended to orient the student to the library, actually are serving to change the library in behalf of the user:

1. The meetings are discussions -- not lectures -- with all participating.
2. Part of the meeting is devoted to a laboratory experience--working on actual problems with real resources.
3. These laboratory experiences are shared --each student reporting on his problem and, in effect, teaching others about the resources that he used.
4. Students use a variety of generic resources to solve their problems, to build up an entire context of resources within which a search is conducted (i.e., not just the card catalog, not just an index -- but catalog, indexes, bibliographies, handbook, etc.).
5. Correlated issues and problems are introduced and discussed--not just media (i.e., a discussion of plagiarism might accompany instruction in the use of

73

microfilm equipment, the workings of interlibrary loan, etc.) since the library does not exist in a vacuum.

6. Students become acquainted through experience with the bibliographic control which traditionally has been part of the library mystique. An attempt is made to diminish the feeling of awe surrounding information sources. NUC, CBI, union lists and shelf lists are theirs as well as ours.

The Appendix outlines a typical workshop for seminar assistants as well as the outline for the first of the in-house programs. As noted, there is no guarantee that the same procedures will be followed again. Moving toward change in library instruction, we know at Wabash that we will change frequently. The only thing that will not change is the laboratory nature of the learning. The students themselves would not have it otherwise.

Students in the seminars undergo a most experiential workshop in the library--a workshop that is structured in advance only as far as having each of the involved professors list research problems that are pertinent to each seminar. The professor is asked to identify information needs in two categories: factual problems and contextual problems. Problems from the January 1972 workshop are included in the program in the Appendix.

These problems become the focus for roundtable discussions and laboratory exploration, with students and faculty sharing their ideas, and with librarians questioning, suggesting, helping to define. Wherever possible librarians may introduce such tools as Winchell, or the L. C. *List of Subject Headings*, and may discuss the suitability of various kinds of resources for specific problems (i.e., almanacs for facts, subject encyclopedia for an overview, handbook for a guide, etc.).

74

There is no homework for the resource person if the librarian wants the workshop to flow naturally. Discussion is hampered by a flat "answer." It is the nomination of possibilities that provides the learning experience for students, that broadens their horizons, and gives them an opportunity to feel real partnership in the learning process. It is a humbling experience for the librarian not to play Authority, but a great one. And one really can't claim to be an authority today-- in the age of information explosion. It is presumptuous.

Part of the orientation plan is to involve students in actual library work. In effect, all become interns at the Reference Desk, for pay, in a program which is a two-way street: providing them with experience in the belief that *doing* aids *learning* (orientation), and providing their fellow students with library service after the Reference Librarian has left for the evening. Teaching, which is showing how, aids learning.

Both seminar assistants and in-house assistants work at the Reference Desk. It is a fulcrum for learning--they on one end, and the teaching Reference Librarian on the other. The problems are real, not at all theoretical since there is a Someone waiting for help.

Responsibilities at the desk include 1) giving reference service and keeping a log of encounters, especially to note difficult problems for the Reference Librarian and make an appointment for her to meet the student client the following day (with feedback on the problem's solution *hopefully* promised to the student assistant at the next class session); 2) shelf - reading the reference collection--so many shelves per night in rotation, with the request that interns examine volumes that are unfamiliar or interesting to them; 3) working on a project of their choice which is both a learning experience for them and a service to the library.

The in-house assistant gives a copy of his learning design to the client and saves a duplicate for the Reference Librarian, a record of his thinking on each problem.

In addition to work in the library at the Reference Desk, in-house assistants are committed to a minimum of five hours per week of bibliographic advising in their living units. The assistants meet with students by appointment or within established "office hours," as announced in flyers of their own design (see samples in the Appendix). Without the library resources, this is a project in which they are actually working as library liaisons, who encourage awareness of and use of the library. We are trying now to evaluate the first semester of work in this project.

I describe the in-house assistants as "designers of learning experiences" for the students who come to them for help. In the reference interview they work with the student to articulate the information problem and select key words which will be the subject headings for search, unless modified by the strictures of vocabulary of the catalog, index, or other resources. They also indicate to the client what kinds of resources would be helpful in solving the problem and why these would be of assistance. The next step is to recommend specific resources for the client to check.

With a design for research in hand, the client can then proceed to the library to work with the resources. When further help is needed, he can go directly to the Reference Desk where the Reference Librarian or one of the trained student assistants will provide assistance.

In these situations, students with some degree of expertise in the use of the library become models for other students, a method of teaching familiar to every parent as well as to psychologists. Jerome S. Bruner wrote that "The earliest form of learning essential to the person becoming human is not so much discovery as it is having a model."[8] Bruner does not deny discovery, but says that the "opportunity to go about exploring a situation," like discovery, "is a necessary component in human learning."[9]

I. *Project Selection* is the preferred assignment. From the periodicals, the student selects journals of interest to them which contain media reviews. On finding a review of interest, he checks the card catalog to see if the library has the resource. If not, he writes a book order card. If he can locate two or three other reviews which indicate the book would be a good addition in terms of the objectives of the collection, the book is generally ordered immediately. If other reviews are not yet available, the card is given to a staff member who checks in later review sources. The student receives feedback about his selection and is notified when the book comes in. Project Selection teaches the student assistants about collection development, the process of selecting materials, and the pros and cons of decision - making. It also helps the student understand the library as a growing mechanism in which he has an active part, and it encourages him to explore journals he might not otherwise know.

II. *Project Awareness* is a public relations activity. The student selects a subject area for a display, supporting his selection with good arguments for its appropriateness, plans the display artistically, and learns how to select what is displayed. So far only Euripides

Tsakarides has been brave enough for this. And as noted, his display was also used as a model to show the in-house assistants how to create what he labeled "little library environments" in their living units.

One of his outstanding displays this year included an invitation to sit down and examine the works on the spot. It was an exhibit of literature on drugs, including relevant Congressional hearings. Placed in the open mezzanine, it flowed through a lounge area where students did respond to the invitation to "read right here." A philosophic statement about the display, in beautiful calligraphy, was a focal point.

Another of Euripides' presentations was a multi-media display dramatizing the black experience. He was aided in planning it by Carl Washam, of Mobile, Alabama, assistant in the freshman seminar on "The Rhetoric of Protest," and Sid Nance, of Cedar Rapids, Iowa, another artistic student. In an area delineated by a huge wrestling mat and deck cushions in salmon, orange, and turquoise, they presented recordings of black literature, poetry and protest, with projections of the new brief black poetry. Fabrics from Africa and slides of Afro-American art gave continuity to the display when records were not being played and interpreted by black students. All students were invited to contribute--the exhibit changed periodically. The Black American flag was displayed, made by Gretchen Wolf Deter, a paraprofessional on the library staff whom Carl Washam dubbed "the Betsy Ross of Wabash."

III. *Project Creation* is the development of either a bibliography or a vertical file collection on a subject of social importance. Consultation with the Reference Librarian is built in, as in an independent study program. One student elected to do a bibliographic essay on works about the American Indian; another, a vertical file collection on Nixon's economic policy; and a third, a bibliography on conscription in the U. S. Two are still unfinished; hours at the Reference Desk speed by since assistants are under instruction to give first priority to students coming for help. But the learning experience will remain, whether or not someone else may finish the bibliography. And the work that has been done may be a beginning for someone else. Perfection is not the point.

Students are encouraged to suggest their own projects for learning about the library. Their eagerness helps to overcome today's deserved radical criticism of detached or irrelevant knowledge. To draw on Bruner again -- "those who study the acquisition of knowledge are surely aware to what extent its acquisition is governed by selective purpose."[10]

Orientation to the library changes hands when students in the seminars encourage their freshmen to meet them in the library for a little serendipity. Seminar assistants in several cases have brought both students and professors to the library to acquaint them with the section where most of the sources used for the courses are, or, in one case, to work on a research problem during actual class time. This is an optimum situation--a library laboratory.

These students are encouraged to prepare for the seminars a bibliography listing of the resources that they found most useful for research in helping the professor plan the seminar, and in their own workshop experience. This involves them in a learning situation since they must review a manual of style, usually Turabian,[11] and present the bibliography professionally, as well as make the selections for it on a critical basis. When they have done this work and it is approved, a member of the library staff cuts the stencils and the work is published under the student's name. He becomes a creator.

In - house students cooperated on a bibliography of the indexes and abstracts they recommended as most useful in the library. As editor, one of them compiled the evaluations of all, which the class published and then distributed to the living units.

This spring, the in-house students also began to compile and write a handbook from the student point of view. It is *their* guide to *their* library, and a record of their awareness of what a library is.

Ben Barnes, of Rochester, Illinois, last fall the senior assistant in the freshman seminar on "The Home Front in World War II," developed a tremendous interest in Congres - sional hearings, influenced by Dr. George Davis, who as his history professor and a government documents enthusiast, was really his model. Ben proved to be so able and so very much interested in the library that I invited him to serve as the assistant in the project for in-house advisers.

One of the areas to be explored by these living unit representatives was our documents collection which, for many reasons, has through the years not been very accessible to students. It's been the old story of an understaffed warehouse--"we have it"--without technique or promotion to get it used properly.

In the last year, all of the indexes from the Constitutional beginning of the United States to the present -- ranging from Poore's and Greeley's to the *Monthly Catalog* and the new cumulative index to Congressional committee hearings--have been isolated and integrated in what we call "Doc's Bar."

As one of his contributions to the in-house project, Ben Barnes developed a working annotated bibliography which is a guide to all these volumes and such supporting handbooks as Schmeckebier, Boyd, and Jackson, and such aids as the valuable catalog *Popular Names of U. S. Government Reports.*[12]

Through this work, sparked by a personal interest, Ben has learned more about access to documents than I know. Today I ask *him* for help. By publishing the bibliography, he has created a project which shares his knowledge and provides guidelines for others. I think this is "a consummation devoutly to be wished."

It is my belief that the key to orientation is being open to experiences which can involve students in actual ongoing library work, work that relates to their own particular interests and personal thrust. It is also offering them measurable results of their efforts--a product or effect they helped create--either a publication or a satisfied client.

As they use resources more broadly, they become more sharply aware of the ingredients of a library, and the feedback from them is very valuable to the library. The librarian becomes much more aware of where his true accountability is--to the student. The Reference Librarian is most keenly aware of this--since the outreach position in public services is where the flack hits. With face to face accountability, in time, the result should be a better library.

At the end of the eight-week period of class discussion and laboratory, in-house reference assistants were asked to suggest things they would do to improve service of any kind in the library, or to improve the environment. The following is the result:

Suggestions for the Library
in its Period of Change and Growth

by Library In-House Assistants
14 March 1972

1. Provide a "how to use" guide for each of the various reference sources, to be located in the proximity of the source.
2. Republish the location guide and self-guided tour, and distribute copies *widely* throughout the library.
3. Provide one or more pencil sharpeners for use in the basement (to be located, perhaps, near the water fountain).
4. Provide several more dictionaries for the basement, located in noticeable, useful spots.
5. Begin the use of raised I.D. cards to facilitate checking out books at the Circulation Desk.
6. Work with projects to make the library a more *personal*, people-oriented place with the help of signs, posters, and a friendly attitude.
7. Provide some form of library guide to explain the roles and jobs of the various librarians and the library staff members.
8. Eliminate the "apples and oranges " question from the library freshman questionnaire: it made the whole survey seem like a joke.
9. Provide a coffee room or lounge where students can relax, have refreshments, and talk. Food machines would be nice.
10. Keep the library open for longer hours. One compromise, based on the financial difficulty of such an undertaking, is to change daily hours from 8 a.m. - 11 p.m. to 9 a.m. - 12 midnight, since very few people actually use the library at 8 a.m.

82

except for classes. In addition, it is requested that the library extend its hours to 1 a.m. the week before, as well as during, exam weeks.

11. Provide a policy statement for all functions of the library, including fines, semester circulation of books, hours, use of phonographs, etc.

12. Place a guard at the door to help prevent the problem of missing books.

13. Have a "library kegger" sometime in April out on the front lawn by and for "friends of the library." It is understood that the general purpose of a kegger is to create interest, to draw attention and people to something. Maybe the library should try it.

Response is the next step.
The Wabash programs, working through model students, do not attempt to reach *all* students directly. This is a strength *and* a weakness. We worry about the unreached. The staff has noted greater use since these programs began, but it is too soon for this to be considered evidence of "results." As statistics are quantitative, a qualitative measure is also needed, a correlation with an improvement in academic achievement. We need more time to know our effectiveness.

Hopefully, however, the outreach of the model students will be greater than just in their seminars or in their houses, with a cumulative library awareness that will spread on campus. As noted in the July & October *Drexel Library Quarterly*, this is intentionally a centrifugal program.[13]

As an indication of their acceptance of the library (orientation to the library), let me, in closing, share with you several responses from students in the in-house program on a questionnaire given to them after the eight weeks of designed experiences.

John Feasel, of Fort Wayne, Indiana, in answer to the question "What is a library?" replied "A big checking account, as opposed to the savings account or warehouse idea."

And in replying to the question "In what way, if any, has your view of the library changed?" (since the start of the project), John continued his analogy:

Most drastic has been the change from the savings account idea ('maybe some day it'll come in handy') to the checking account -- one always being used, handy and convenient in the transactions of knowledge. Teach people that, using fair practices, they can enjoy years of credit. All they have to do is put in a fair amount of their own work as a deposit.

From Bruce Ong, of Elkhart, Indiana, comes this definition of a Library: "A storehouse of information, books, periodicals, and services. It is a storehouse until it is used. Only then is it a library."

Mark Nicolini, of Mishawaka, Indiana, projected that

the library is what the individual is willing to make of it--it knows no limits or boundaries. The only confines are people's lack of learning desire. For the curious, it can be a new world--but only if they allow it to be.

Responding to the question "What is essential in an effective library environment?" Mark felt that "most fundamental is an atmosphere of encouragement: i.e., questions will be grappled with by staff, although not necessarily 'answered.' Libraries need not guarantee 'success' but they have a *commitment to help*."

84

"Help" is a verb that denotes personal concern and meaningful action. In the language of situation ethics, help is an action in the present, thought out in loving concern, as a bridge to the future.[14]

Orientation which involves students in a total library experience on a one-to-one basis, rather than in an assembly line of isolated exposures, cannot be anything but a commitment to help--a sane approach to young people questioning shallow educational leadership and objecting to a shoddy and unconcerned world.

It is these young people on which the Council on Library Resources has practiced the laying on of hands, confirming them as "the reservoir of national leadership to take us through the decades ahead."[15]

APPENDIX I

Library Project   January 15, 1972
Wabash College
                 WORKSHOP SCHEDULE

9:00 a.m. How to attack factual problems: three
           assistants from Fall 1971 seminars
           will try to find the answers to ques-
           tions put by this spring's seminar
           leaders -- Andy Barnes, Keith
           Nightenhelser, Chuck Ransom.

           Exercise in finding answers to fac-
           tual questions which the leaders
           have submitted as being typical of
           their seminars. The assistants will
           hunt; the librarians will assist.

10:30 a.m. Report on snags hit so far. The li-
           brarians will point out how to use
           major categories of reference works
           (indexes, bibliographies, card cata-
           logue, and the like) to avoid the
           snags.--Thompson, Millis.

           Return to the exercise on the factual
           questions.

1:30 p.m. Round-robin. Each assistant puts
           one of his factual questions to the
           group, as a simulation of what the
           work at the Reference Desk can be
           like.

2:00 p.m. Each assistant meets with his seminar
           leader to discuss the authorities--
           the authoritative resources--of their
           seminar, in order to (a) demonstrate
           the process of making judgments about
           sources of information, to (b) test
           the resources of Lilly Library in
           particular, and to (c) make a pre-
           liminary statement of the scope of
           the seminar.

86

2:45 p.m. Brain-storming on a "core curriculum" and its relationship with Freshman Seminars and the Library Project.--Frederick.

3:15 p.m. The services of the work room: CBI, Union List of Serials, shelf list, LC catalogues and NUC volumes, and the like.--Millis.

Arranging a work schedule for the Reference Desk: the assistants should have their class schedules in hand.

End around 4:00 p.m.

The mid-term workshop will be held on Friday afternoon, March 3, starting at 3:00.

Please return the critique forms to Mr. Strawn on Monday, January 17.

Library Project Workshop, January 15, 1972

Factual questions for 9:00 a.m.

For detailed consideration:

1. What kinds of careers generate published autobiographies and what ones don't?

For casual consideration:

2. Find five definitions of time.

3. With whom does the technical distinction between *langue* and *parole* start?

4. Who said it? Where was it said? Why was it said? What was the response?

April 24, 1916
"Irishmen and Irishwomen: In the name of God and of the dead generations from which she receives her old tradition of nationhood, Ireland, through us, summons her children to her flag and strikes for her freedom.

"Having organized and trained her manhood through her secret revolutionary organizations, the Irish Volunteers and the Irish Citizen Army, having patiently perfected her discipline, having resolutely waited for the right moment to reveal itself, she now seizes that moment and, supported br her exiled children in America and by the gallant allies in Europe, but relying in the first on her own strength, she strikes in full confidence of victory."

F.S. 7 APPLIED GENETICS: MOLECULAR ADAPTA-
TION. Cole, Doemel, Butler.

1. Where can I find a procedure for the
   assay of aldolase activity in bacteria?
2. Where can I find a theoretical discussion about liquid scintillation counting?
3. Where could I find a listing of all the
   papers published by Thomas Brock or his
   associates?
4. How can I find references published from
   1960 to the present about the development of the chloroplast in Chlorella?
5. How do I find research reports of gov-
   ernmental agencies--NIH and EPA?

F.S. 8 AMERICAN AUTOBIOGRAPHIES.
Frederick, Kissling.

1. What kinds of careers did individuals
   pursue which generated published autobiographies? Rank the top 10 or so in
   order -- approximately. What kinds of
   careers, incidentally, do not seem to
   generate published autobiographies?
2. Find -- and list -- the top 10 (approx.)
   best-selling, "best-received" autobiographies written in the last ten years.
3. Define and show the distinctions, if
   any, between the following: biography,
   autobiography, novel, memoirs, reminis-
   cences, fictional autobiography.
4. What are the two or three bibliographical sources most indispensable to any
   study of American autobiographies?
5. Find two reviews with contrasting in-
   terpretations and/or evaluations of
   any autobiography of your choice.
6. Who was Vida Scudder and what has been
   written by and about her?

F.S. 9   LOCAL HISTORY
         Fertig, Stepp

1. If the property of Wabash College were placed on the tax rolls, approximately what annual property tax would the college pay?
2. From a study of indexes to 2 or 3 Indiana histories (including Carmony and Barnhart) derive a statement about what leads a state historian to mention Crawfordsville or Montgomery County.
3. Compare the book-length publications of Maurice Thompson listed in Russo and Sullivan, *Seven Authors of Crawfordsville*, with the Wabash Library holdings. Check with the Public Library to see if it can supply anything Wabash cannot.
4. [If Archives are open...] How much help would the Wabash archives be in supplying pictures for an illustrated account of "Wabash during the First Decade of the Administration of President Tuttle"?
5. Which of the articles listed under Indiana in a volume of *Reader's Guide* (pick your volume) can be consulted in the Wabash library?
6. How many votes did McClellan get and how many did Lincoln get in Montgomery County in 1864?
7. Find data to substantiate or refute the "impression" that Montgomery County was a "rich" county in 1880.
8. Why is the morning ceremony on Commencement Day called Baccalaureate?

F.S. 10   WHERE ARE YOU? WHAT TIME IS IT?
          McKinney, Thoms.

1. Prepare a bibliography on Newton's concept of absolute space and time.

2. Compare Erwin Schrödinger's and Max Born's interpretation of the wave function. Document the sources.
3. Who originally developed the following theories and concepts: valence, vortices, and *vis viva*. In what source are these theories first mentioned?
4. What scientific perspectives have developed from the thought of Heraclitus and Parmenides?
5. Find a scholar who believes that space comes into existence as a particle is set in motion. (Does space exist independently of motion?)
6. Find an article, monograph, or book which discusses the concept of space in the works of Rembrandt or Vermeer.
7. When did the theories of relativity and quantum mechanics first appear in American newspapers?

Speech 9. RHETORIC OF PROTEST.
            O'Rourke, Washam.

1. How many definitions can you find of rhetoric and protest? You are expected to use the various dictionaries in the library, but in addition to these consult the various writers on rhetoric and protest for their definitions.
2. Develop a list of synonyms for rhetoric and protest that would be useful in a search of the catalogues and indexes in the library.
3. What 10 articles in the last 20 years of the *Quarterly Journal of Speech* would you recommend to students of the Rhetoric of Protest for background reading?
4. What recordings are available in the library that would be useful in the Rhetoric of Protest course?

5. What journals in the library will members of the class find useful for their research. List at least five of them and cite one article from each that you feel pertains to the course.
6. List magazine articles, newspaper stories and editorials on the following events:
   Assassination of Martin Luther King
   Riots in Watts
   The Berrigans' arrest

Humanities 8 LINGUISTICS.
            Strawn, Carpenter.

1. Where will we find a classification of African cultivated plants by type and by origin?
2. Find a couple of photographs that will let Amadou Taal talk for three minutes in Wolof about what is familiar to him.
3. What teaching materials do we have for African languages?
4. Find a schematic for showing kinship. What is a cross-cousin?
5. What has been published within the last decade on the relationships between language and biology?
6. What 19th - century work in linguistics has received new attention since 1960?
7. What is the significance for linguistics of Ferdinand de Saussure? Is Wade Baskin's translating ability trustworthy?

Lilly Library
Wabash College

IN-HOUSE REFERENCE ASSISTANTS
SCHEDULE & OBJECTIVES
WINTER & SPRING 1972

OBJECTIVES

1) FAMILIARITY with basic types of library
resources and certain models.
2) PLANNING HOW to develop greater student
awareness of library services, and of
potential for self-development there
3) GIVING ASSISTANCE to fellow students in-
house, channeling them to the Reference
Librarian first for help, and gradually
gaining enough confidence to help them
individually.

PART I

MEETINGS

Week of: at: 1-2:30 o'clock

1) January 17 (Jan. 18), read & do *Library
Skills; a Program for Self-Instruction.*
N.Y.: McGraw-Hill, 1970, Chapter 1.
Class pattern: Introductory presentation
(30 minutes), exploration in the library
("library laboratory" -- 30 minutes), and
discussion (return to Goodrich Room to
share findings--30 minutes)
Class topic: *Library Research and Research
Ethics*, guest consultant: Professor
Peter Murphy.
2) January 24 (Jan.25), read *L.S.*, Chapter 2.
Class topic: *Encyclopedias, Handbooks,
Dictionaries, Companions.*

3) January 31 (Feb. 1), read *L.S.*, Chapter 3. Class topic: *Card Catalog and Other Bibliography.*
4) February 7 (Feb. 8), review and completion of problems. Class topic: *Use of the LC Dictionary of Subject Headings.*
5) February 14 (Feb. 15), read *L.S.*, Chapters 4,5. (Allow a little longer for the programmed instruction this time than in previous assignments) Class topic: *Indexes and Other Specialized Information Sources.*
6) February 21 (Feb. 22), read *L.S.*, Chapter 6, through "Almanacs and Yearbooks," p. 135, and in the library look up and examine each book for greater familiarity. Class topic: *The Library Mystique Revealed!*
7) February 28 (Feb. 29), read *L.S.*, Chapter 6, from "Atlases and Gazetteers" through "Indexes to Literature in Collections." Locate each book held in our collection and examine it for greater familiarity. Class topic: *Government Documents,* tour of the collection and the Government Documents Index Bar, guest consultant: Professor George Davis.
8) March 6 (March 7), internship with Mrs. Millis at the Reference Desk at arranged times. Class topic: *Interlibrary Loan,* discussion of interlibrary loan procedures, demonstration of microfilm equipment, guest consultant: Library Intern Mike Wilson.
9) March 13 (March 14), as above. Class topic: *Developing Awareness,* guest consultant: Senior Euripides Tsakarides, "Posters and other awareness devices," problems relating to desk duty, filling in gaps.

SPRING VACATION MARCH 18-26

Next 6 weeks: Reference Duty in Lilly Library, 6 - 8:30, 8:30 - 11 p.m., as scheduled (optional).
In-House Reference Duty: a total of five hours per week, according to individual's schedule (required).
Keep Reference Log of "problems" you need to refer to Mrs. Millis. Follow the "Guide for Reference Assistants." Arrange for substitute from the group or ask Andy Barnes to take your place if you are ill or any emergency keeps you from your responsibility.

"Feed - back" on your problems will be either via Andy or via shorter sessions bi-weekly.

10) Week of April 24 (date by class vote), dinner at Mrs. Millis'. Evaluation of program.

Andy Barnes, as tutor, coordinator and record - keeper, and Gretchen Wolf Deter, as reference assistant, will help Mrs. Millis and Mr. Thompson evaluate your work and commitment to your responsibility to Part I, to determine your eligibility to continue with Part II. Satisfactory evaluation will mean payment of the second check for $50.00, which signifies your appointment to do the in-house advising for the weeks between spring vacation and commencement. You will be paid at the rate of $1.85 an hour for the work at the Reference Desk, and an attempt will be made to distribute work as evenly and fairly as possible.

Charlotte H. Millis
Reference Librarian

Log of Research

Researcher:

Date:

Problem #__ of above date:

Place advice was rendered: Living unit ( )
                            Library   ( )
                            Other _____

I. Statement of the problem as client and I
   conceive it:

II. Key words we identify for our research
    in library sources:

        Our nominations: With help from *Dic-
                                tionary of Subject
                                Headings*, thesauri,
                                & other dictionaries

        1.   1.
        2.   2.
        3.   3.
        4.   4.
        5.   5.
        6.   6.

III. Resources I think will help us:

Generic resource ("family name"); Ex.: *Index*	Specific resource; Ex: *which* index(es)?	
1.	1.	7.
2.	2.	8.
3.	3.	9.
4.	4.	10.
5.	5.	11.
6.	6.	12.
		(abbreviate)

IV. Record each citation on a separate 3X5" slip, to be found at the card catalog (unnecessary for the log). You may have several citations in each category above.

V. Brief evaluation of this problem of research--why "successful" or not:

Notes

1. Quoted at end of article in *Improving College and University Teaching*, 16 (Autumn, 1968), p. 275.
2. Frank Goble. *The Third Force: The Psychology of Abraham Maslow*. (N.Y.: Grossman, 1971).
3. Nat Hentoff. "From Nat Hentoff's Luncheon Speech," *Top of the News*, 26 (November, 1969), p. 75.
4. Albert Camus. *The Misunderstanding*. Translation unknown.
5. Council on Library Resources. *Fourteenth Annual Report*. (Washington, D.C.: Council on Library Resources, Inc., 1970), p. 14.
6. Michael Polanyi. *The Tacit Dimension*. (N.Y.: Doubleday, 1967), p. 91.
7. Jerome Bruner. *The Relevance of Education*. (N.Y.: W.W. Norton & Co., Inc.), p. ix.
8. *Op. cit.*, p. 70.
9. *Idem.*
10. *Ibid.*, p. xiii.
11. Kate Turabian. *Student's Guide in Writing College Papers*. (Chicago: University of Chicago Press, 1970).
12. Bernard A. Bernier, Jr. and Charlotte M. David. *Popular Names of U.S. Government Reports: A Catalog*. (Washington, D.C.: Library of Congress, 1970).
13. "Integrating Library Instruction in the College Curriculum," *Drexel Library Quarterly*, 7 (July & October, 1971), 365 ff.
14. Joseph Fletcher. *Situation Ethics. The New Morality*. (Philadelphia: The Westminster Press, 1966).
15. Council on Library Resources, *op. cit.*, p. 14.